# Re-entry!

Striking Parallels
Between
Today's News Events and
CHRIST'S SECOND
COMING

# JOHN WESLEY WHITE Ph.D.

Foreword by Billy Graham

# Re-entry

Special Crusade Edition
**WORLD WIDE PUBLICATIONS**
1313 Hennepin Avenue
Minneapolis, Minnesota 55403

To my wife
Kathleen

# Contents

# FOREWORD

The theme of *Re-entry,* the second coming of Jesus Christ, is urgently needed in the preaching of the Church today. I am a social activist in the areas of war, poverty, pollution, racism, illiteracy and crime. I am doing everything I know to do, to get these ravaging scourges under control. But no one can read the facts and be unaware that things are getting worse instead of better. And they will continue to get worse and worse until Jesus Christ comes again to institute His program for peace and prosperity on this earth.

John Steinbeck told me before he died that he could see no hope for America unless we had a catastrophe. A catastrophe we may have, but I believe Jesus Christ is coming again and that He will save us from nuclear extermination. We have now reached the point where only He can. That is why the Church has a theology of hope. Winston Churchill asked me seventeen years ago: "Young man, can you give me any hope?" I said to him as I say to all: "Jesus Christ is our hope!"

The author of this book has been one of my Associate Evangelists since 1964. He has been of invaluable personal assistance to me in the area of research. During his time with me, he has traveled to a hundred countries, preaching the Gospel from Minneapolis to Moscow and from Montreal to Melbourne. In one of his recent crusades, held in Sioux Falls, South Dakota, over 2,000 inquirers came forward to make decisions for Christ. He is a compassionate and compellingly persuasive evangelist.

John Wesley White is a native of Canada, where he played ice hockey and was vice-principal of a high school. Called into evangelism, he trained at the Moody Bible Institute and Wheaton College in Illinois. Moving to the British Isles, he did graduate research at Queens University and Trinity College in Ireland, and finally Oxford University in England from which he earned the Doctor of Philosophy degree. In addition to his evangelistic ministry, he serves as Chancellor of Richmond College in Toronto.

As an author, Dr. White has written *Everywhere Preaching the Gospel,* an account of the work of my associate evangelists, and *Mission Control,* messages he has given around the world. *Re-entry* was first published last year, and when I decided to use it to give to our television viewers, Dr. White updated it.

*Re-entry* is a series of addresses which Dr. White actually gave in the world-famous "Peoples Church," where he regularly worships with his family, when he is home. These are not evangelistic sermons which he would preach in a crusade, but essentially a teaching rather than a preaching of the Gospel, and this, obviously, only on one doctrinal theme. Their uniqueness, and therefore their chief merit, lies in the fact that they dwell almost entirely on the parallel between Biblical signs which were specifically prophesied concerning the second advent of Jesus Christ, and actual events which are currently transpiring all around us. Not all will agree with Dr. White's interpretation of some of the precise events which accrue around the second coming of Christ, but all will be moved by the message.

Probably no Gospel theme apart from "Ye must be born again" is more relevant today, and I preach on some facet of this subject in virtually all of my crusades. Our world is filled with fear, hate, lust, greed, war and utter despair. Surely the second coming of Jesus Christ, His "re-entry," is the only hope of replacing these depressing features with trust, love, universal peace and prosperity. For it the world, wittingly or inadvertently, waits.

BILLY GRAHAM

# INTRODUCTION

As the astronauts rode aloft in the Apollo XI from their Cape Kennedy launching, Mrs. Armstrong was asked how she felt. "I wish it were splashdown rather than blastoff," she sighed. Not until "re-entry" took place could she really relax. But as her husband Neil went away, so he returned.

The turbulence of our times is reaching the breaking point. Only the "re-entry" of Jesus Christ can alleviate the escalating anxiety of a troubled world. He promised, "If I go away, I will come again." And whereas it is man's "Endeavor" (the command ship of Apollo XV) which takes man to the moon, when Jesus Christ returns, it will be God's turn to remove His people from terrestrial terrors to celestial triumph. The "re-entry" of the Russians cosmonauts of Soyez 11 issued in tragic death, gloom, and temporary defeat for a disappointed Soviet Union. The "re-entry" of Jesus Christ will issue in triumphant life, glory, and eternal victory for an appointed Church universal.

*Time* magazine carried two references to Christ's "second coming" during the epic summer of 1969. One was in the account of man's landing on the moon. It asserted that the only event which could command larger worldwide headlines would be "the second coming." Jesus Christ is coming again!

The second was in a statement by that fascinating if tragic figure, the late James Pike. He reckoned that Christianity, to be viable and tenable in our highly sophisticated world, simply must demythologize itself of the teaching of the second coming of Jesus Christ. Divested of hope, this man, with so many likeable traits, died a dreadful death in the kind of barren wilderness in which he had been living for many years. As the press put it, he was literally going through "torments trying to find himself and failed." An ironic postscript to James Pike's disavowal of the second coming was provided by the

*Time* cover story of June 21, 1971, entitled "Jesus Is Coming." *Time* wrote: "Few spiritual Odysseys . . . are as circuitous as that of Christopher Pike, the younger son of the late Episcopal Bishop James A. Pike. In 1967 he began combining marijuana highs with nonstop television watching: 'TV and grass, that was my god,' he says. Then came acid, Eastern religion and Bible reading — while stoned. Recalls Chris: 'One day I saw Ted Wise speaking in Sproul Plaza at Berkeley. He was the first intelligent Christian I ever saw.' Soon thereafter, he made a commitment: 'I just said, "Jesus Christ. I'm going to give myself to You and nobody else." Nothing happened, but I knew. I knew He had reached down, and I was saved.' Now Chris lives in a trailer near Reno, studying religious books and working on a library of religious tapes. 'The old Chris Pike died back there,' says the Bishop's son. 'I'm a new creature.'" To meet Chris Pike is to meet a vibrant youth, powered by the expectation that "Jesus Is Coming." His prayer is that the facts of Christ's coming and of His coming again may have a similar effect on millions of lost and frightened people of our generation.

"We are saved by hope," wrote St. Paul. A woman whose family wealth runs into the eight figure bracket tells me that her fifteen-year-old daughter is mainlining heroin because she insists that she and her generation were born under a mushroom cloud, and are without hope. I pray that she and her millions of disillusioned contemporaries will read Chris Pike's story and follow his example.

In the following chapters I have elected to quote profusely from the Scriptures on the one hand and current events on the other. I felt that rather than put forward my own views significantly, I would prefer to point to what I consider astonishing parallels between contemporary news reports and the Bible. The reader must be the arbiter by weighing the facts and drawing his own conclusions.

JOHN WESLEY WHITE

# Chapter One

# Theology and the Coming Christ

Five more days and the most celebrated Presidential Inauguration of the century would be taking place. Already the awesome responsibility of the most powerful office on earth was settling down on to the shoulders of the young President-elect. At his father's West Palm Beach mansion to finalize his plans for the New Frontier, he might have invited a fellow statesman, a speech specialist, a tension-relieving entertainer, or an enterprising relative to join him for golf. But no, he had something else on his mind.

Walking with him to the beige Lincoln to take the drive to the Seminole Golf Course was a clergyman. And sliding through opposite doors into the front seat of that Continental convertible were indubitably the world's two most charismatic figures. Reflectively and with sober concern, John Fitzgerald Kennedy turned and looked searchingly into the eyes of Billy Graham: "Billy," he asked with even more than his usual candor, "would you tell me about the second coming of Jesus Christ? I don't know much about it!" And as the car moved slowly out on to that Florida roadway, the evangelist shared with his friend Scripture after Scripture which answered the query. Then there was a second question. "What does my church teach about the second coming of Jesus Christ?"

A fleeting 46 months later, Cardinal Cushing would give the answer to that question before the television cameras of a planet in deep mourning and over the coffin of an assassinated President. The words were neither those of Billy Graham nor Pope Paul VI — but those of another Paul: an ancient Apostle writing from a Roman jail to Thessalonian Christians: "we would not, brethren, have you ignorant concerning those who are asleep, lest you should grieve, even as others who have no hope," goes the Douay Version of the 1 Thessalonians 4:13-18 passage. The Boston Archbishop further recited, "for the Lord Himself with cry of command, with voice of archangel, and with trumpet of God, will descend from heaven; and the dead in Christ will rise up first. Then we who live, who survive, shall be caught up together with them in the clouds to meet the Lord in the air, and so we shall ever be with the Lord. Wherefore comfort one another with these words."

Newspapermen around the world in their shoptalk for years have referred to "Second Coming Type" as the largest headlines they are capable of engaging. According to the Gallup Poll, 3.64 times as many Americans as voted for Richard Nixon in the 1968 Presidential election believe in the second coming of Jesus Christ. Approximately the same number of people as voted for Hubert Humphrey indicated that they did not know whether or not they thought Jesus Christ would return to this earth at some future point in history.

The second coming is good news. For ours is as anguished an age, as it is angry. It is both ironic and paradoxical that man should be ripping in half as he is being catapulted upward, slingshot into space by a sophisticated scientism, while he is being savagely sucked from beneath by the woes of warism, the stalking suffocation of pollution, proliferating poverty, raging racism and the ultimate weaponry which beckons impending annihilation. Schizophrenically-split through the middle, he yearns to get glued together again. So he snatches at any straw of hope.

Multitudes who have rejected Christianity or are ignorant of its experience are turning increasingly to the prophetic prognosis of astrology. It's the "in" thing for the jet set. "Psychic Phenomena: Communication from Beyond?" mesmerizes a national TV audience in mid-1971. In his craving to see forward, man turns backward to an ancient Persian cult, astrology, and diligently pores over its omens that appear in two out of every three American newspapers. Moderns will engage in star gazing or crystal gazing. If they can't escape stark reality by going to the horses, there is the horoscope. Psychiatrists are beginning to complain that the clairvoyants and the Cassandras are doing them in. UFO'ers and ESP'ers; Yoga masters, occultists; voodoo priests and sorcerers; gurus and psychic seers with their spooky seances are having a field day. The younger crowd of course prefer LSD and STP, for man is a chronic tripper. He must have a psychedelic experience, even though hallucinogenic drugs may induce him to jump insanely out of a skyscraper window, or from a bridge.

Man simply must have hope: future hope. That is why Bible prophecy in general and specifically the second coming of Christ is so relevant to the human situation today. Twelve hundred delegates from 32 countries gathered for the Jerusalem Conference on Bible Prophecy in what *Newsweek* for June 28, 1971 labelled "the first conference of its kind since A.D. 50." It was assembled under the co-chairmanship of the longtime Editor of *Christianity Today*,

theologian Carl F. H. Henry who made it clear that
the gathering had been convened to highlight current
events, as they related to the second coming of Jesus
Christ. "We live already in the last days," stated Dr.
Henry and, "The very last of those days is soon to
break upon us."

Prophecy, that is, predictions of future events,
occupies approximately one-quarter of all Scripture.
The teaching of the second coming of our Lord is
dealt with some 1,845 times in the Bible, 318 of
these being in the New Testament. The return of the
Lord is the dominant theme of 17 Old Testament
books and one epistle in the New. In fact, 7 out of
every 10 chapters in the New Testament make reference to the second coming. Whole passages of the
last half of the Bible are given over exclusively to
its discussion. It is clear from the Scriptures that
Christ is not only to be the subject but the object of
our preaching. We are to proclaim not only the
Christ of the second coming, but the second coming
of Christ. "The doctrine of the second coming,"
wrote C. S. Lewis, "may be to some people intoler-
ably frustrating. . . . Perhaps you were going to get
married next month; perhaps you were going to get
a raise next week; you may be on the verge of a
great scientific discovery; you may be maturing great
social and political reforms. But *now,* of all mo-
ments," asserted Lewis, "Christ may come again."

Merv Griffin was interviewing Billy Graham recently before the millions of television viewers who
were watching his late night show. Mr. Graham, as
always, made the claims of Jesus Christ unmistakably
clear and vitally relevant. Whereupon Mr. Griffin
reflected the interest of people around the world by
thinking out loud: "I've often wondered what would
happen if Jesus came back again!" Mr. Graham
assured him that Jesus Christ was indeed coming

again, and proceeded to explain what the Bible teaches on this timely theme.

Overzealous soothsayers from time to time deliberately disobey Jesus Christ and predict dates for a forthcoming divine appearance, often bringing into disrepute one of the most precious and potent doctrines of the Christian Church. Archbishop Trench translated Mark 13:32, "if I were not God, as well as man, even I should not know the day nor the hour." Jesus was emphatic that we should not set dates for doomsday. The late Elizabeth Steen, a 28-year-old Richmond, California, housewife brought thousands of her fellow Californians to a state of near panic by predicting that on April 14, 1969, a series of catastrophic earthquakes would destroy the coastal area of California. Kooks, cultists and hippies gave the portent maximum mileage with a rash of pop songs like "Where Can We Go When There's No San Francisco" and "California Earthquake." Curt Gentry thrived on the proceeds of his *The Last Days of the Late Great State of California*. When the "doomsday" arrived, 10,000 people (reportedly) gathered at 5:10 a.m. in downtown San Francisco and when nothing happened, many made obscene gestures in the direction of God. Being in that region at that time, I resolved never to play God as a date-setter.

In Hertford, England, a local newspaper notice read, "The world is definitely coming to an end on Wednesday, December 11, 1968; at noon precisely. A full report will appear in this newspaper next Friday." When the Friday came, there was no doomsday to report, so the editor re-ran the article with his own editorial postscript, "We're still here!" A feature article in the *Canadian Magazine* describes how a group had "seen the Holy Virgin in the sky," and that she would be returning to St. Bruno, Quebec, on October 7, 1969. These isolated instances of delusion must not be permitted to cause us to avoid the proclamation of Christ's return.

God the Father, said Jesus, knows when He will send His Son back. I coach a hockey team whenever I am home in Toronto during the winter months. My three eldest sons play together on a forward line. One night there was a dispute between the referee and the timekeeper over when the game would end. "The game is over!" called out the referee. "Two minutes to go!" asserted the timekeeper, adding, "My father is the Commissioner of this league and we're playing according to his time." The game went on for two more minutes. This world is running on, not according to the timekeeping of scientists, statesmen, or well-meaning prognosticators, but according to the plan of God the Father.

Without hope, our world cannot go on. "What oxygen is to the lungs," observed Emil Brunner, "such is hope for the meaning of life." "While we live this life," said St. Paul, "we hope and wait for the glorious denouement of the great God and of Jesus Christ our Saviour." Our Canadian Ambassador to Egypt, Herbert Norman, commits suicide with a scrawled note in his pocket: "I have no option. I must kill myself, because I cannot live without hope." *Reader's Digest* affirms that to be happy, we must have someone to love, something to do, and something to hope for. Christ provides all these for the believer, but only if we rest in His promise to come again. Lord Montgomery asks of Mr. Eisenhower via Telstar, "Can you give any hope?" Mr. Eisenhower prescribes a way out, which, if man misses it, will lead surely ". . . to Armageddon." President Nixon is right in stressing that what the peoples of the world need today is new hope. Hiley Ward of the *Detroit Free Press* calls for theology books on "hope."

*The Greening of America* offers an exciting prospect. But the only way it can be effected is by the return of Jesus Christ.

The world hopes for the best but Jesus Christ offers the best hope. An old year goes out with the newspaper headline: "A Year of Tragedy Saved by a Space Spectacular." Writers everywhere are speaking of a world in tragedy. Can it be saved? Only by a space spectacular: the return of Jesus Christ. The director of the National Aeronautics and Space Administration remarked, "Man has started his drive out into the universe, the beginning of a movement that will never stop." He is right. Someday, Jesus Christ will come and free us forever from all gravitational drag: moral and mortal. When the Russians were about to launch their first cosmonaut into orbit, they announced that the venture would be a "final rehearsal for a cosmic journey." Mankind is in a final rehearsal for a cosmic journey, surrounded as he is by events which according to Scriptural forecasts are harbingers of an eternal cosmic journey for the true Church of all ages. This turning toward "Space: A New Direction for Mankind" (as a new book title expresses it) can add a whole new dimension to living.

Father Clifford Stevens, a Roman Catholic clergyman, proposes a new look at theology in the light of the aerospace age. He points out that according to Einstein's theory, men who travel at or near the speed of light will experience a deceleration of time, so that a man in an ultra-fast ship will age only a few months, while his family and friends back on earth are living through decades and generations. Some scientists claim that when man can travel faster than electricity, literally "time will be no more." The aging process will cease. The Russians now announce that terrestrial fuel for space travel

will soon be obsolete, for they have perfected a
process of utilizing celestial nitrogen as fuel for
space travel. The physics of eternity and infinity are
breaking in upon us. St. John the Apostle wrote in
his sunset years, "Beloved, now are we the sons of
God, and it doth not yet appear what we shall be:
but we know that, when he shall appear, we shall be
like him; for we shall see him as he is" (1 John 3:2).

Just what basis do we have for entertaining such
a euphoric prospect? This is not a new question. St.
Peter foresaw that it would be asked! "In the last
days there will come men who scoff at religion,"
anticipated St. Peter, "and they will say: 'Where now
is the promise of his coming? Our fathers have been
laid to their rest, but still everything continues exactly
as it has always been since the world began'" (2
Peter 3:3, 4, NEB).

No Christian should permit himself to be denied
for a moment the assurance that Jesus Christ is coming back. In fact, we are really only Christian, if we
believe that our Lord is returning. It was Jesus Himself who put forward that bedrock promise, "Set
your troubled hearts at rest. Trust in God always;
trust also in me. There are many dwelling-places in
my Father's house; if it were not so I should have
told you; for I am going there on purpose to prepare
a place for you. And if I go and prepare a place for
you, I shall come again and receive you to myself,
so that where I am you may be also; and my way
there is known to you" (John 14:1-4, NEB).

At this point, Thomas the doubter interrupts in a
manner typical of anyone who is thoughtfully curious: "Lord, we do not know where you are going,
so how can we know the way?" (John 14:5, NEB).

Jesus replies with the familiar words which obviously apply to His coming again: "I am the way;
I am the truth and I am life: no one comes to the

Father except by me" (John 14:6, NEB). To accept any of Jesus' words as authoritative means we must accept them all. None are more relevant than His promise, "I shall come again."

When we were holding a Crusade in Brisbane, Australia, we were taken to the place where Douglas MacArthur had his headquarters during World War II. He had come from the Philippines, where, prior to leaving, he had waded waist deep out into the Pacific and dramatically exclaimed to the onlooking Filipinos, "I shall return!" For long months and years, those island dwellers waited under cruel oppression. They were reassured from time to time by underground pamphlets, leaflets from overhead air raids and unjammed radio reports, that eventually they would be emancipated. As the five-star General promised, "I shall return," so he did.

This world is under siege, as John Kennedy articulated, from the forces of "tyranny, poverty, disease and war." Only the return of Jesus Christ can ultimately resolve these problems.

On the mausoleum where the body of Martin Luther King, Jr., lies, is the inscription, "Free At Last!" When Jesus promised "the Son sets free," He was referring not just to liberty in Christ here on earth, where at times even the most devout feel trapped or strapped into impervious situations. He pointed to the ultimate prospect of complete and eternal freedom, made possible at His coming, "to wit, the redemption of our body."

Plain as Jesus had made the promise of His coming again to His disciples, at the time of His ascension, they still did not seem to grasp its significance. An aggregation of 500 of them stood looking upward on that historic occasion. As the Lord ascended, He detected their consternation and sent messengers of assurance: ". . . suddenly two men dressed in white stood beside them and said, 'Men of Galilee, why are you standing here looking up into the sky? This very Jesus who has been taken up from you into Heaven will come back in just the same way as you have seen him go'" (Acts 1:10, 11, Phillips). As He went away, so He will come again. As He ascended, so He will descend to receive His Church into eternal glory.

When anyone reads or hears of this for the first time, it understandably sounds mysterious. "Listen!" St. Paul assured the Corinthians, and "I will unfold a mystery: we shall not all die, but we shall all be changed in a flash, in the twinkling of an eye, at the last trumpet-call. For the trumpet will sound, and the dead will rise immortal, and we shall be changed. This perishable being must be clothed with the imperishable, and what is mortal must be clothed with immortality. And when our mortality has been clothed with immortality, then the saying of Scripture will come true: 'Death is swallowed up; victory is won!' 'O Death, where is your victory? O Death, where is your sting?' . . . God be praised, he gives us the victory through our Lord Jesus Christ" (1 Corinthians 15:51-57, NEB). What a resplendent passage to have been read at the funeral of Winston Churchill!

Nor was this teaching the private preserve of St. Paul: a sort of hobbyhorse which was distinctively Pauline. All of the apostles proclaimed this event as the zenith of history. The writer to the Hebrews exhorted Christians always to live as if in "a very little while, He that cometh shall come, and shall not tarry" (Hebrews 10:37, Phillips). St. James was concerned that believers should maintain a posture of vigilance, ". . . patient and stout-hearted, for the coming of the Lord is near" (James 5:8, NEB). St. Peter explained that any number of trials can simply be treated as trials of triumph since they will issue in ". . . praise and honour and glory at the appearing of Jesus Christ" (1 Peter 1:7).

"Now, my children," wrote the aging St. John with tender love, "dwell in him, so that when he appears we may be confident and unashamed before him at his coming" (1 John 2:28, NEB). John seemed to feel that Jesus Christ would possibly come again during his lifetime, based probably on the words of Jesus concerning him to Peter during the post-resurrection interlude: "If it is my wish for him [John] to stay until I come, is that your business, Peter?" (John 21:22, Phillips). The octogenarian John, as he concluded recording his Revelation of Jesus Christ on the Isle of Patmos, replied to our Lord's assertion, "Yes, I am coming very quickly!" by saying, "Amen, come, Lord Jesus!" (Revelation 22:20, Phillips).

Jude traced his doctrinal belief in the return of our Lord to antiquity, quoting ". . . Enoch also, the seventh from Adam, prophesied . . . saying, Behold, the Lord cometh with ten thousands of his saints, To execute judgment upon all, and to convince all that are ungodly among them of all their ungodly deeds which they have ungodly committed, and of all their hard speeches which ungodly sinners have spoken against him" (Jude 14, 15).

Alexander Maclaren aptly noted, "The primitive Church thought more about the second coming of Jesus Christ than about death or about heaven. They were not looking for a cleft in the ground called a grave, but for a cleavage in the sky called Glory. They were not watching for the 'undertaker,' but for the 'Uppertaker'." They felt that man's chief end was to get right with God or to be left when Christ returned. Winston Churchill's favorite American song was, "Mine eyes have seen the glory of the coming of the Lord!" That was the vision of the ancient apostles: one which gave them dynamism and direction.

All the great catholic creeds of the Church give a climactic place to the return of Christ. To hear once or to repeat daily the Apostles' Creed is to know the impact of those resounding words, "from thence He shall come to judge the quick and the dead," or the Nicene Creed, "He shall come again with glory to judge both the quick and the dead." The Presbyterian Confession of 1967 hails "the hope of His coming." Augustine used to reason that when Jesus commanded, "Lazarus, come forth," He did so to limit the resurrection to the one man Lazarus; but in that great day, He would say, "Come forth," and the cemeteries of the world would yield up their Christian dead at His behest.

The Reformers were greatly inspired by the prospect of Christ's coming again. "I live," exclaimed Martin Luther, "as though Jesus Christ died yesterday, rose again today and were coming again tomorrow."

Every English-speaking Christian will forever be indebted to Tyndale for his Bible. He once described the motivation for his ministry as springing from the realization that "Christ and His apostles warned us to look for Christ's coming again every hour."

As Bishop Ridley was being burned at the stake in front of Baliol College, Oxford, he exclaimed, "Let us with John, servant of God, cry, 'Come, Lord Jesus!' "

Calvin, Bohler and Spangberg referred often to the coming again of Jesus Christ. Two centuries later when the Wesleys were rekindling the flame that the Reformers had spread, Charles Wesley made appeal to the return of Christ as the climactic goal for all Christian service. He thematically included it in 5,000 of his 7,000 hymns reflecting the emphasis which his brother, John, gave it in his preaching.

The nineteenth century was what the Yale historian, the late Kenneth Scott Latourette, called the "Great Century of Christian Missions." Jonathan Edwards, whose theology and edition of the *Diary of David Brainerd* did so much to inspire the founding of the early missionary societies, had been, in the mid-eighteenth century, a watershed evangelist, theologian and philosopher. He inspired new interest in the second advent of our Lord. Frontiersmen like William Carey, Henry Martyn and Alexander Duff, zealous students of Edwards, were drawn to the ends of the earth with the Gospel largely because they believed that a pre-condition of Christ's return was, in the words of our Lord, that "this gospel of the kingdom shall be preached in all the world for a witness unto all nations; and then shall the end come."

Some of the really eminent missionaries of their century, such as William Patton and David Livingstone, who heralded the Gospel in the dark and remote spots of the earth, and prominent churchmen in the enlightened lands of Europe and North America began to give a growing place to the Scriptural teaching of our Lord's return. In England, Archbishop Trench held that the "second coming is possible any day; impossible no day." The voice to the masses, Charles Haddon Spurgeon, told his hearers that "the coming of the Lord is far more the hope of the Church than any remedial process, evolution or progresses among mankind."

Queen Victoria refused to break precedent with tradition and go to hear Spurgeon, a non-Anglican, expound, although her curiosity almost got the best of her on one or two occasions. But her Chaplain, Dean Farrar, was as passionate a believer in the second coming of Christ as Spurgeon, and so was Queen Victoria. On the first anniversary of the accession of Edward VII to the throne of England, during the service in Canterbury Cathedral, Dean Farrar finally revealed how the late Queen, after hearing one of her chaplains preach at Windsor on the second coming of Christ, spoke to the Dean about it and said, "Oh, how I wish that the Lord would come during my lifetime." "Why does your Majesty feel this very earnest desire?" asked the Dean. With appropriate emotion, she replied, "Because I should so love to lay my crown at His feet."

Queen Victoria had heard of Christ's return at her Coronation in 1837. At the Coronation of Queen Elizabeth II in 1953, I happened to be in London. It was an unforgettable moment when the Archbishop of Canterbury, Dr. Geoffrey Fisher, extended to her Majesty the crown in the historic ceremony which states, "I give thee, O Sovereign Lady, this crown to wear, until He who reserves the right to wear it shall return."

In nineteenth-century America, the Episcopalian, Bishop Phillips Brooks, was the voice of orthodoxy in proclaiming that "the coming of the Lord has been the inspiration of the Christian world. The power of any life lies in its expectancy." There were indeed innumerable crude and miscalculated distortions of this doctrine, especially on the American frontier, as over-zealous and unbalanced prophets announced dates, called out colonies of tarriers and made all sorts of weird predictions with regard to the second advent. To the sophisticated, these foreboding and disillusioning predictions of dates and places tended to bring the return of Christ into ludicrous ridicule. Nonetheless, the nineteenth century of Christian revival and world evangelism rode on the crest of a realization that there was a Mount Everest on the horizon, because Jesus Christ was coming again.

As the twentieth century began, many of the most

able thinkers were no longer believers in the actual return of Christ. They resurrected the ideas of Plato, More, Fourier, Owen and Bellamy, insisting that man himself would eventually achieve Utopia on this earth and that human nature was perfectible. W. E. Henley, who died in 1903, wrote: "I am the master of my fate: I am the captain of my soul." Optimism was in vogue. As a spokesman of modernist Christianity, Harry Emerson Fosdick was later to articulate, "The kingdom is not something which comes down from heaven, but which is to be worked at among men."

But World War I came and Englishman Sir Edward Grey lamented, "The lamps are going out all over Europe." It was a new era: the reason historians begin the twentieth century with 1914. War, according to humanists, was to have been abolished, but during the next 30 years it wiped out as many lives as had perished in wars during the previous 800 years. In fact, the theories of man's nature being reformable had been exploded. It was now quite evident, as Dwight D. Eisenhower pointed out, that unless there was a moral regeneration throughout the world, mankind could, on any given day, wake up in the dust of an atomic explosion. But no prospect of a moral regeneration appeared. Man could not seem to bring himself to a state of repentance. Instead, he seemed to freeze in panic while conditions worsened.

In 1860 the French scientist, Pierre Berchelt, had stated that "inside of one hundred years of physical and chemical science, man will know what the atom is. It is my belief that when science reaches this stage, God will come down to earth with His big ring of keys and will say to humanity, 'Gentlemen, it is Closing Time!'"

One of Europe's most eminent churchmen, Pastor Niemoeller, entered the 70s completely pessimistic

regarding man's ability to survive. As Harold Lindsell, editor-in-chief of *Christianity Today*, points
out, man without God cannot survive. And as ministers of the Word of God, "we are called upon to
pronounce judgment on a society that is doomed;
a society that cannot be saved until the coming of
Jesus Christ." Thank God, Jesus is coming again.

For the last 25 years, in the words of President
Nixon, the world has been a "powder keg that needs
to be defused." Divisions are deepening. Walls are
heightening, and tensions sharpening. As Jean Paul
Sartre, the French existentialist, points up, "There
is no escape from the present dilemma." "How shall
we escape," asked the writer to the Hebrews, "if we
neglect so great salvation?" (Hebrews 2:3).

The hope of ultimate salvation is the coming again
of Jesus Christ. Fifty million more Americans believe in the afterlife today than twenty years ago,
despite the decline in church attendance. *Psychology
Today* for June, 1971, polls its half million readers
and reveals that a majority of Americans actually
"yearn" for eternal life, just as did the rich young
ruler. There is a new looking to the celestial for the
manifestation of the Son of God. *Time* devotes its
religion section to "the theology of Hope," a revised
phenomenon of German theologians. Conceptions of
Christ's coming again vastly differ, but it is the one
theme which defies neglect in an age dominated by
pessimism. The *New York Times* carries on its front
page the forebodings of the British author, C. P.
Snow, who believes our world is beleaguered with
insoluble problems. Each year he feels the pessimism
deepen. He leaves the impression that civilization is
about to be abolished unless there is a divine intervention. Walter Lippmann puts it, "For us all the
world is disorderly and dangerous, ungoverned and
apparently ungovernable." Who will restore order?

Who alone can govern this world? The answer is Jesus Christ. Thank God, He is coming again!

So it is with considerable interest that we listen to Father Joseph Christie on "The Sacred Heart Hour" speak from the prophecy of Joel on our Lord's return; that we read the statements of the Mayor of Nazareth on the occasion of the visit of Pope Paul VI regarding "the second coming of Christ"; of Eugene Carson Blake, who writes, "I want you to know that I still believe as I was taught in my youth, that the second coming of Jesus Christ is an important and vital part of the full rounding of the Christian faith"; of the late Kenneth Scott Latourette, former President of the American Historical Society, who replied to a questioner, "I believe that our Lord may return at any time and bring this present stage of history to an end. That may well come between now and the year A.D. 2,000."

The young too are on to it, as on pop radio the lyrics of: "Everybody Get Together" go: "When the One that left us here, returns for us at last"; or "He's coming down to get you! Are you ready?" "Yes, we're ready!" is the chorused reply. In mid-1971 Sydney Poitier stars in the newly released film "Brother John" which everywhere is featured as a message picture on "The Second Coming of Christ." And after a year of media-jamming news items on the gory Charles Manson case, the most publicized of those who had worshiped him as Messiah, Linda Kasabian, turns to Jesus Christ as her Savior and Lord, longs for His return, and is reconciled to her husband from whom she had been estranged, together to work in the ranks of the Jesus people.

Nor is it out of character that news commentator Paul Harvey should express his delight on one of his national newscasts that the Gospel song which has moved back to the center of the stage by force of current events is:

> When the trumpet of the Lord shall sound
> And time shall be no more.
> And the morning breaks eternal, bright and fair;
> When the saved of earth shall gather
> Over on the other shore,
> And the roll is called up yonder, I'll be there.

# Chapter Two

# Science & Technology and the Coming Christ

Pierre Berton in his best seller, *The Comfortable Pew,* alleges that in every battle between the Scriptures and science since Copernicus, the Bible has lost. This is untrue. For one thing, science has man today propped on the precipice of doom. But it is the Bible which reveals the salvation of Christ, the only viable option open to man. What Berton might have said is that religious zealots construct a superstructure of hypotheses on the alleged foundation of the Scriptures; that students of science construct what W. R. S. Thompson, Director of the Commonwealth Institute of Biological Control, Ottawa, in his introduction to Charles Darwin's *Origin of the Species* (New York, 1959) calls, ". . . those fragile towers of hypotheses based on hypotheses, where fact and fiction intermingle in an inextricable confusion." It is when the highly-biased defenders of these two fabricated bastions clash, that the sophistries of the latter seem often to prevail intellectually over the frequent ingenuousness of the former. Notwithstanding, it is refreshing to read in *Time* magazine that "reputable scholars now believe that the New Testament account is reliable history." And as its history is reliable, so are its prophecies.

Equally refreshing in times like these is that the most charismatic of the astronauts, Colonel Frank Borman — indeed, the most popular American ever to visit the Soviet Union — can say, "I believe now that man can do anything he wants, technically," and yet introduce from the moon orbit the creation account from Genesis 1. He believes in technology. And he believes in the Bible. Without this combination man cannot survive, let alone thrive. Britain's Prince Philip has never been known as an enthusiastic evangelist. But this year he has been speaking out. Recently in Toronto with poignant solemnity he cautioned that unless "the high priests of science" were prepared to subordinate their discoveries to an orientation which would be dominated by faith in God, there would cease to exist a basis of belief for man's survival on this planet. This is a sober observation, stating that if scientists ignore God, man will lose his life. "In many ways," laments Mark Hatfield, "God has been replaced by technology and we worship at the altar of materialism. When we are in trouble, we rely on the Technological Fix instead of Faith."

God's books of science and Scripture never contradict each other. I have never seen a shred of evidence to support the comparably fallacious conjectures that the findings of science are sinister or that it is no longer viable to hold to the fidelity of the Scriptures. Francis Bacon, as one of history's prominent scientists, in his *Advancement of Learning,* put forward his own views on this: "Let no man, out of a weak conceit of sobriety, or an ill-applied moderation, think or maintain, that a man can search too far or be too well studied in the book of God's Word, or in the book of God's works . . . but rather let men endeavor an endless progress or proficience in both." For a thousand years of Medieval Ages, western man was prepared to believe anything religion did or said. For a hundred years there have been those who have been prepared to believe anything a student of science says, actual or apocryphal. But today, as we quest for truth, we like to look hard. Science fiction is going out of style because science is revealing so much that once could be thought of only as fiction. On the other hand, as Chancellor Solandt of the University of Toronto points out, science does not solve the basic problems of living. "The nineteenth century witnessed the loss of faith in God and the kingdom of heaven," reasons the New York pundit, Eric Hoffer: "*we* are witnessing the loss of faith in man and the kingdom of heaven on earth."

All of which leads us to say that man needs a new order. Science can facilitate, but not fulfill. God intends to meet our needs. His program is to send back His Son. I think that science and technology are currently confirming conditions which the Scriptures state would prevail at the time of Christ's coming again.

The prophet Daniel in the fourth verse of his last chapter predicted that at "the time of the end ... knowledge shall be increased." The Hebrew translation of these words could be much stronger, i.e., "A sudden knowledge explosion will occur at the time of the end." Surely on this basis we must be at least in the fringe zone of "the time of the end." Currently, knowledge is doubling every ten years, and printed materials every fifteen years.

Forty-six percent of all Americans between 18 and 21 years of age — over 8 million — are in university or college today, double the number of ten years ago. Education is a top priority. Without it, no person or people can live well.

Eighty percent of all the scientists in history are alive in the world today. There are 15,000 different scientific journals being published regularly, many with a world-wide circulation. Seventy percent of the medicines used today have been developed since World War II. Something as ordinary as a credit card will soon have 420 items of information on it.

The computer, hardly two decades old, is taking over the thinking role of millions of human brains. There is a new one which can perform 55 billion transactions in one second. When Apollo XIII ran into trouble 205,000 miles from earth, scientists working with computers figured out the correct return flight path for the crippled craft in just 84 minutes. Working with pencil and paper in the pre-computer age, it would have taken one man 1,040,256 years. Today, we are told that whole wars could be fought by computer.

In from three to eight years, says Marvin Minsky, M.I.T. scientist, we will have a machine with the general intelligence of an average human being. I mean a machine that will be able to read Shakespeare, grease a car, play office politics, tell a joke, have a fight. At that point the machine will begin to educate itself with fantastic speed. In a few months it will be at genius level and a few months after that its powers will be incalculable. According to how it is used, the computer could facilitate the turning of this world into a paradise or a holocaust.

*The Chicago Tribune* peers from 1971 into the future to predict Americans living in modular plastic homes, ordering their meals from a computer, spraying on their clothing and working only for enjoyment. Television sets will have, as standard equipment, converters to tape programs for later viewing, and also may be connected into a central computer bank, so that programs on any theme the viewer may wish to watch can be selected at will. As he travels, wrist watch TV sets will be as common as transistor radios are today.

One of the most fascinating advances in technology, highlighted in the Apollo moon landings, is the planting of the laser beam reflector on the moon surface to get an exact measurement of its distance from the earth. First discovered a decade ago, the laser beam of light is revolutionizing many areas of science. It concentrates tremendous energy into a pinpoint of light and generates intense heat. Metals can be welded by it, machine guns and rockets fired by it. In medicine, laser beams are sent through glass fibers to treat growths in inaccessible parts of the body, and detached retinas are rejoined to the eye by their use. In space communication, laser beams are being used to bring television pictures from outer space in seconds, and in industry they have vaporized coal into gas, making hitherto uneconomical coal seams workable.

Stockpiles of information are not in themselves either good or bad. It is the use to which such knowledge is put that matters. "A wise man will hear, and will increase learning," exhorted Solomon in his first chapter of Proverbs, predicated on the realization that "The fear of the Lord is the beginning of knowledge..." (Proverbs 1:7). It is well-known today, however, that God, to many moderns, is neither the beginning nor the end of knowledge. He is simply ignored, if indeed it is admitted that He exists at all. As Paul wrote to the Romans, "Thus, because they have not seen fit to acknowledge God, he has given them up to their own depraved reason" (Romans 1:28, NEB).

Why is it that just when men are reaching the heights of knowledge, it is imperative that Jesus Christ come again? Because, as Paul wrote to the Corinthians, "...'knowledge' breeds conceit..." (1 Corinthians 8:1, NEB), and in the words of the ancient Jeremiah, "Every man is brutish in his knowledge..." (Jeremiah 10:14). We are only just now beginning to realize this. A team of scholars was commissioned by the United States Government to prove that education lessens crime. To their complete surprise and disillusionment, the team announced three years and several hundred thousand dollars later that as an outcome of their research, they had discovered that education, in fact, escalates crime. Man's need for the return of Christ is in direct proportion to his increase in knowledge.

Another condition Daniel foresaw would prevail at the "time of the end" was that "many shall run to and fro." The prophet was not referring to manual jogging being stepped up to sprinting, but to the whole realm of human transportation. Travel in prodigious vehicles at incredible speeds would carry men from one point to another in ever-shortening times. In Isaiah 31:5 we read the prophecy that "as birds flying" so would be the defense of Jerusalem. Who could read this and not relate it to the events of today or the much more astonishing prospects of tomorrow? Who, a century and a half ago, could have imagined a world in which the steam engine, then the internal combustion engine, the electric motor, the jet engine, and now the thermonuclear fueled motor would propel man across land and sea, and up through the air, as is happening today? Russia's new supersonic airliner, the TU144 with Aeroflot, conveys 130 passengers 4,000 miles at 1,500 miles per hour: twice the speed of sound. Boeing's jumbo jets can carry up to 500 passengers at once. When one is able to have an early morning service in Sydney, Australia, and that same night preach the evening service in a church in Johannesburg, some 8,000 miles away, one realizes how far we've come since the Wright brothers first test flew an aircraft in Carolina in 1904. Travel is getting to be a way of life. Pierre Berton, interviewing a movie actor, Dennis Morse, on television asks him how he deals with his frustrations. "I solve my problems geographically," Mr. Morse replies. Living in New York, he flies annually some 250,000 miles, having been to London ten times and to California twelve times during what had been a typical year.

Throughout the Scriptures, we are told repeatedly that the coming of Christ will be accompanied by the sound of a trumpet. A physics laboratory in Upper New York has demonstrated that a large steel ball can be hoisted and held aloft in mid-air by focusing an intense beam of high-frequency sound waves under the ball. The ultrasonic sound was of too high frequency to be detected by the human ear. This electronic phenomenon is the kind of thing that could happen when Christ returns to rapture (Latin "to snatch away") His Church into the celestial. Those whose faith is in Christ, who are alive or deceased, will respond to the trumpet call. To those without faith, the only realization will be that true believers in Christ are suddenly gone.

Melba Moone, made famous by her role in "Hair," is currently singing "There's a new world a-comin'" in one line of which she belts forth, "There's a new 'voice a-comin'." She is right. The "new voice" will be "The Lord Himself shall descend from heaven with a shout" and Christians of the ages "shall be caught up together to meet the Lord in the air."

From cover to cover, the Bible refers to the fact that the coming of the Lord is immediately to be followed by a judgment. Secularists used to smile when it was stated that "God shall judge the secrets of men by Jesus Christ"; or, as Jesus Himself put it: "by a man's words shall he be justified and by a man's words shall he be condemned. But informed people are reluctant to smile anymore, for it is now possible through sophisticated instrumentation, to

extract from solids, conversations which were made
nearby, at a given time in the past. It may presently,
for example, be possible to recover from a contiguous stone, the actual voice of Moses, as he replied
to God at the burning bush. The vibrations are still
there, somewhere, if they can be located, isolated and
extracted. Every sound leaves a sound track. Think
of it! God summons the judgment and someone protests that he never said, did or thought a certain
thing which shows up on his record. So Gabriel, say,
goes from the Court and brings in "exhibit 'E' " and
a stone cries out the truth. Telepathists are now convinced that every thought also leaves its vibration
trail somewhere. If men can do this, what can
God do?

A news item in mid-1971 throws light on this
matter of the judgment. The Soviets are now survey-
ing the United States on three of every four days,
from a satellite network which is so thorough that
they have photographs which will reveal the numbers
of shingles on houses in every part of the United
States. It makes sense out of a statement like, "all
things are naked and opened unto the eyes of Him
with whom we have to do."

"Is man's flight into space to be found in Scriptural prophecy?" is a question currently widely asked.
Assuming that one or more of the astronauts who go
to the moon are Christians, whatever would happen
if the second coming of Christ were to occur while
they were aloft in space? Jesus Christ foretold that
"With a trumpet blast he will send out his angels,
and they will gather his chosen from the four winds,
from the farthest bounds of heaven on every side"
(Matthew 24:31, NEB). The majority of Bible scholars with whom I am acquainted think that this reference relates to the "Revelation" of Jesus Christ and
will occur seven years after the rapture. Hence there

would be time for large numbers of His "chosen" to be out in space somewhere. It seems to me it could also happen in measure at the time of the rapture. Angels therefore will fulfill the behest of our Lord to gather the saints together wherever they are.

Mrs. Madalyn Murray O'Hair may have attempted to undermine the spiritual dimension of space travel by hoisting a black flag against the Bible reading of the astronauts, but Mrs. Frank Borman had the last word in that exchange. "O to have all our prayers answered so completely," she rejoiced as the men of Apollo VIII splashed down, adding, "Look at the prayers around the world that pulled this thing through!" The astronauts, the parents and the wives of Apollo XI let it be known to the whole world how dependent on prayer they all were. Commander Borman puts it, "The more we learn about the wonders of our universe, the more clearly we are going to perceive the Hand of God." When Apollo XIII was lost in space, many commentators reckoned that never in the modern history of man had so many prayers been offered for the physical safety of three persons.

There are Bible students who have been suggesting for some time now, that Jeremiah's reference to men who "mount up to heaven," is a description of man's ascent into space. I do not know. But I am sure that God is not surprised, though we may be, that man now has traveled 24,630 miles per hour; has been 233,000 miles from the earth; has seen the moon's far side; has lost total contact with the earth, temporarily; has been for the first time outside the earth's gravitational pull and been in that of the moon's; has actually landed on the moon and walked on a heavenly planet; and has looked down from the heavens at the earth from that celestial vantage point.

As President Nixon puts it, the heavens have now "become a part of our world." With the launching of Russia's Salyut in June, 1971, a space station as large as a railroad station finds its home in the sky; and, for the first time in the history of technology, men actually ascend into the heavens to live.

Ray Bradbury (author of *Martian Chronicles*), featured by Walter Cronkite as the greatest of the science fiction writers, reckons on CBS-TV that interplanetary travel will drive men back to God and the Church because of the sharpened loneliness it will impose upon them. It also seems to me that if man cannot cope with lostness on this earth, what will he do when he begins to traverse the heavens? The Christian hope is that Christ will come again and liberate believers forever from terrestrial limitations.

Several other Biblical incidents are rendered credible, if not comprehensible, by man's venture into space. It used to be asked: how could Jesus walk on water? Is it not relevant today to reason that if a son of man — Russian or American — can walk in space, the Son of God could walk on the Sea of Galilee? The *Eagle* descended to the moon and then ascended to orbiting *Columbia* with Neil Armstrong and Edwin Aldrin and then soared out into space. Is there not a resemblance in this to believers being caught up to meet their Lord in the air? If it took 7,500,000 pounds of thrust (the power of 500 jet fighters) to get a Saturn V rocket with an Apollo aboard off its Florida launching pad en route to the moon, is it not logical to believe that "when the Son of Man cometh" the faith He shall find in the hearts of believers will far exceed this, and therefore free them from the earth's gravitational pull? If, as our Lord said, faith can remove a mountain, it can surely take a man to heaven! The pop singer's lyric of mid-1971 becomes a possibility: "Lord, I wanta go to heaven, but I don't wanta die!"

Something else which this trip to the moon brings up, and especially because the three astronauts read from Genesis 1, is the prophecy of the ancient Joel that there would be a turning of ". . . the moon into blood, before the great and the terrible day of the Lord come" (Joel 2:31). Jesus repeated this prophecy and made it unmistakably clear that this event would be in connection with His "coming" and prior to the end of the world. St. Peter spoke of it on the Day of Pentecost, and in Revelation 6:12 we see a description of its future fulfillment: "I beheld . . . and the moon became as blood." But why Genesis 1? Because there we read that when God commanded the sun to shine by day and the moon to shine by night, He did so first of all for "signs" and then "to give light upon the earth."

In four of the major prophetic references of Scripture the fact of the moon being turned into blood is mentioned. This seemed absurd and, to all but unwavering Biblicists, an embarrassment to Christian believers a generation ago. But today it is no longer preposterous. I read in the *Australian* an article by a Russian astrophysicist, who was rationalizing a current reddening of the moon, and the chemical process which caused it. A Socialist Prime Minister of Britain poses another possibility: "I would gladly let the Russians have the moon and paint it red." This was made in response to the Russian leader who avowed that the Communists would spray the moon with red dust. Another discussion by pundits is that, in fact, a fiercely fought war may take place by earthlings as they battle for possession of the moon, a mass carnage which would turn it into a bloody battlefield. Although these are all mere possibilities, they do demonstrate the tenability of Biblical predictions in the unfolding panorama of current events.

In the same prophecy our Lord states that ". . .

the sun will be darkened . . . the stars will fall from
heaven, and the powers of the heavens will be
shaken" (Matthew 24:29, RSV). This may or may
not coincide with St. Peter's prophecy of finality in
which he predicts that ". . . the day of the Lord will
come as a thief in the night; in the which the heavens
shall pass away with a great noise . . ." (2 Peter 3:10).
In any event it may be thought of as a part of that
whole series of consummation activities for which the
world in particular and the universe in general are
destined. Ray Bradbury stated on CBS to Walter
Cronkite that the sun is due eventually to blow up,
or be blown up, in a huge celestial explosion. "The
Day the Earth Caught Fire" and "2001: A Space
Odyssey" show the cinema-goer the terrible and
magnificent aspects of future activity in space. Regarding "the stars fall from heaven," *The Indian-
apolis Star* displays a photograph taken by the
Palomar Observatory in California with an account
of an explosion in the heart of a galaxy of stars
which is currently cutting a swath sixty billion miles
wide, and rolling forward at the rate of twenty million miles an hour. So the universe is by no means
static, as once was thought.

With regard to St. Peter's description, "a great
noise," it is not insignificant that Fred Hoyle, Cambridge astronomer with few peers in his field, is now,
with his whole influential school of thought, of the
opinion that the universe came into existence with
a "Big Bang." A team of astronomers, taking their
data from a radio telescope one mile long, has announced that they suspect that they may be hearing,
across the millions of light-years, reverberations of
the "big bang" with which all creation came into
existence billions of years ago. This sheds light on
the integrity of the Genesis opening: "In the beginning God created the heavens and the earth." And

as it came into existence, so it will go out — with a "Big Bang." Does this not sound amazingly similar to the phrase, "a great noise"? It is the prevalent theory among astrophysicists today. From a geophysical point of view, *Time* magazine quotes two eminent geophysicists as stating that "if the magnetic field of the earth continues to run down at its present rate, the earth has less than 2,000 years until Doomsday." In another issue of *Time*, an M.I.T. professor reasoned that it is entirely possible that at any time an asteroid could well collide with the earth and turn it back into a blob of molten lava.

St. Peter's prophecy, "the elements shall melt with fervent heat" (2 Peter 3:10), is possibly easier for a scientifically-oriented society to comprehend today. A generation ago, it seemed to many to be ludicrous, if not quite comic; but not now. Not for those who have visited Hiroshima or Nagasaki; nor for those who are familiar with thermonuclear weapons. It has been suggested by Hebrew scholars that when Sodom and Gomorrah were being destroyed, God may have used an atomic explosion. For when Lot's wife, whom Jesus told us to remember, ". . . looked back . . . she became a pillar of salt" (Genesis 19:26). The word for "salt" might be rendered "ash." An interesting parallel: those who turned and looked back at the Nagasaki conflagration, turned into ash. Inexplicably, others with them who fled with their coats over their heads escaped untarnished. Nikita Khrushchev detonated a fifteen megaton H-bomb a decade ago, which was five times the explosive power of all the bombs used in World War II combined, and in the estimation of the Russian scientists, 2½ times as hot as the center of the sun. As the *Sydney Herald* put it, "Scientists have now discovered Doomsday fire!" Former President Johnson warned that if another World War breaks out, it inevitably will be, as compared with all the previous wars of history, like tossing a firecracker up against the surface of the sun.

St. Peter in that passage on "the Day of the Lord" (a passage in which he makes room for a series of destructive events by stating that "a day is with the Lord as a thousand years") clearly indicates that ". . . the earth also and the works that are therein shall be burned up" (2 Peter 3:10). Lester Pearson tells the students of Queens University that the annihilation of all life on this planet would now take precisely thirty minutes, and he is not optimistic that man can escape his own proclivity for self-extermination. Before his death, DeGaulle of France doubted if man could survive because he has in him the seeds of his own self-destruction. The Unitarian Professor Linus Pauling reckons that there are now enough thermonuclear explosives stockpiled to equal twelve one-ton bombs for every acre on earth.

I descended into an American Minuteman Missile silo some time ago and saw how one of a thousand of these readied I.C.B.M.'s could be triggered off and within a matter of minutes turn a city halfway around the world into what the Commanding General described as an apocalyptic lake of fire and brimstone. Terrifying enough reading was provided a few years ago by Herman Kahn's *On Thermonuclear War*. Now David Inglis, the senior physicist at the Argonne National Laboratory in Washington, in his *Unless Peace Comes* warns of a hydrogen bomb wrapped in cobalt which can annihilate all life in the Northern Hemisphere, where 3 billion people live. Nobel prize winner, Harold Urey, for two decades now, has feared a thermonuclear chain reaction which could not be stopped.

Is it any wonder that Jesus solemnly cautioned of a time of great tribulation ". . . such as has never happened from the beginning of the world until now, and will never happen again" (Matthew 24:21, Phillips)? So terrible would be the maelstrom of woe that Jesus declared "if that time of troubles were not cut short, no living thing could survive" (Matthew 24:22, NEB). Bible scholars have calculated from Scriptural prophecy that approximately one-half of the human race will be wiped out by apocalyptic wars and woes, but, thank God, just when man is about to annihilate himself and everything living is about to be demolished, ". . . for the sake of God's people those days are to be shortened" (Matthew 24:22, Phillips) and ". . . as lightning flashes across from east to west so will the Son of Man's coming be" (Matthew 24:27, Phillips). What person with a heart could ever have misgivings over the second advent of our Lord, for were He not to come, man would annihilate himself.

"Every man, woman and child lives under a nuclear Sword of Damocles," warned John F. Kennedy, "hanging by the slenderest of threads, capable of being cut at any moment by accident, or miscalculation, or by madness." That slenderest of threads will be severed by "man's inhumanity to man," but God be thanked, that all-exterminating thermonuclear Sword of Damocles will be caught in mid-air by the returning Saviour. Red-lettered headlines in the *Toronto Star* read "Man and World Folds!" They would, but for the advent of our Lord.

Science and technology are largely where they are today because of frenzied efforts by the nations to research, invent and mass produce weapons which are capable of vanquishing their adversaries: "all sorts of armour," is the Biblical prophecy. Jesus said in answer to His disciples' question as to " 'What will be the signal for your coming and the end of this world?' 'You will hear of wars and rumors of wars' " (Matthew 24:3, 6, Phillips). During the pre-World War period, classical Christianity came perilously close to ignoring this ominous portent. The hard facts since have driven men to face grim reality. John F. Kennedy called the world in general and America in particular to "a long twilight struggle, year in and year out . . . a struggle against . . . war itself."

The price for American defense in men alone is a current 3,450,000 men in the armed forces. At this moment armaments are costing the world annually an astronomical 204 billion dollars per year, which, as U Thant pointed up in mid-1971, is "an intolerable waste of resources." That is 40 percent more than is spent on education and more than three times the amount invested in public health. Put bluntly, man is three times as desirous — on the average — to kill as he is to render healing to his fellowman. We talk of universal brotherhood, but there seem to be more hoods than brothers emerging. According to Senator Mark Hatfield, there is currently the equal of 15 tons of T.N.T. for each of the 3½ billion humans on earth.

In Caesar's day, when our Lord prophesied "wars and rumors of wars" prior to His return, it cost 75 cents for the Roman army to kill an enemy soldier. By the first World War this had risen to $15,000; during the second World War to $30,000; during the Korean War to $50,000; and now in Vietnam it costs the Americans just over a million dollars for every Viet Cong they kill. Is it any wonder that Barry Maguire captivated youth in the 1960s with his pop rendering of "Eve of Destruction"; or Meryle High, the youth of the '70s with: "This world is headed for destruction, like Ancient Rome; this world is doomed; Jesus, take a hold and lead us through"?

I have been in Red Square, Moscow; and from the bottom to the top of South Vietnam; in north India and central Africa, and everywhere the most impressive hardware were the military weapons: "all sorts of armour." The feature of Mr. Nixon's Inauguration address in 1969 was peace, but he was careful to say that America would keep itself militarily as strong as needed and for as long as needed. Russia responded in 1970 by announcing another six percent increase in its armaments allocation for the ensuing year. America in turn is obliged to step up its 10,000 nuclear bombs to 17,000, just to keep pace. Says Melvin Laird: In the last five years the Russians have trebled their nuclear megatonnage.

"All sorts of armour" seems to be descriptive of Russia's military equipment. The Russian leader calls in American reporters and tells them of their hovering space bombs (the *Chicago Tribune* says the Soyuz goal is this); gigaton bombs, cobalt bombs, death ray bombs, neutron bombs, and chemical bombs. British intelligence warns that the Russians are concentrating on hovering space platforms from which they can trigger bombs. It is also known that they have surrounded North America with nuclear bombs aboard a network of submarines, with a Fractional Orbit Bombardment System, capable of reaching momentarily any North American city. And from 1961 to 1971 Russia's nuclear-powered submarines had increased from 3 to 90, their output being in a 2-1 ratio over the Americans. Joining the nuclear submarine race in mid-1971 were the Red Chinese.

Senator Albert Gore now claims that the Russians have 22 nuclear weapons pointed at each of the 50 largest U.S. cities. Eugene Wagner of the American Civil Defense program reckons that it would cost Americans 13 billion dollars to try and salvage 75 million people in a first exchange in a limited thermonuclear war. It sounds strangely Biblical and at the same time terrifyingly realistic for the Smothers Brothers to feature the pop song, "What Do You Do, When There's No Place to Hide!"

Toronto's First Unitarian Church used to be a place where it was only fashionable to talk about world peace. Now it is the rendezvous for vitally relevant discussions on survival of at least a few people in a nuclear war. Perhaps our most distinguished Canadian protagonist of peace is our former Prime Minister, Lester Pearson, winner of a Nobel Peace Prize. He commands a world audience for his sharply pessimistic warnings, given on BBC-TV, on the terrifying prospects of nuclear war through accident or miscalculation: a sort of "Fail Safe" omen.

The situation is not helped when according to NBC, Israel now has nuclear stockpiles, and the Arabs are determined to have the same. With their oil reserves, who could seriously doubt their capacity to buy what they may not be able to make for themselves? Alan Adelson writes in *Esquire* of the amazing ease with which the small nations of earth can procure shipments of uranium isotopes, the key ingredient for manufacturing atomic bombs. And China has now detonated a three megaton bomb, reaffirming her resolve to conquer the world, and giving evidence that in two years she will be able with modern I.C.B.M.'s to deliver her bombs to any point on earth. According to *Look* the majority of Americans expect eventually to have to enter an all-out war with China. In this respect, President Nixon has said, "Time is not on our side!" Richard Bueschel reveals in his book, *Communist Chinese Air Power*, the dramatic growth of the Chinese air force; it is now third in the world. Who can doubt Red China's intention of wiping out any number of foreign "imperialists" and "revisionists" to gain world domination, since it has been revealed that an estimated 65 million Chinese' have been exterminated since the Communist drive to power: all this to consolidate an atheist regime!

According to the *Toronto Star,* while the Russian leaders were signing peace pledges with the leaders of Egypt and Canada in May, 1971, they were simultaneously completing "300 holes. Each hole is 100 feet across and 25 feet deep; and it contains a smaller, deeper hole, 30 feet wide and going down 120 feet. In most of the holes, the Russians planted huge missiles, each capable of carrying a nuclear warhead equivalent to 25 million tons of T.N.T." (All the bombs of World War II combined amounted to 3 million tons of T.N.T.)

It used to be held in contempt that the last book in the Bible should predict that one-third of the population of the earth would be killed in one horrible holocaust. No one smiles any longer, for today one bomb alone could kill over three-quarters of the world's people. Paul Harvey deliberately recommends that people read the book of Revelation if they want to see what modern weaponry can and may well be used to do. Otto Klineberg of the Sorbonne in Paris, in introducing Nigel Calder's *A Scientific Forecast of New Weapons* (15 essays written by scientists in 6 nations) states frankly, "The material presented in this volume is terrifying." It describes in sickening detail the laboratory research leading to nuclear, thermonuclear, biological and chemical silos and stockpiles of weaponry. Also there are environmental bombs: psychological drugs which can change completely the activities, interests and reactions of whole nations. All of these are packaged and deliverable through underseas, overhead or robot warfare; war by computer; attacks by spacecraft: *ad infinitum nauseum.*

We sometimes wonder why Russia talks so much

about anti-nuclear ban pacts. As Lester Pearson says, Russia alone in a conventional war could place ninety divisions in the battlefield, the U.S.A., thirteen. Whether or not one believes the Bible is a source of prophecy for today, if he walks through Red Square on any May Day, he cannot do otherwise than say: this is a display of "all sorts of armour." Despite peace propaganda, nearly every government in the world seems to be saying to its industrialists, "Beat your plowshares into swords, and your pruning hooks into spears," as the ancient prophet Joel predicted (Joel 3:10).

I have met people who will get hung up on prophecies like the one in Ezekiel where it states that when the Russians invade Israel (the word "ascend" for going "down south" sounds like a military airlift), and are defeated in the most devastating military demise in history, they will have wooden equipment. People don't get hung up on the fact of this being about to happen, for current events in the Middle East demonstrate how the stage seems to be getting set for such an encounter. But they do get hung up on the statement that when the battle is over, "they that dwell in the cities of Israel shall go forth and shall set on fire and burn the weapons . . . with fire seven years: so that they shall take no wood out of the field, neither cut down any out of the forests; for they shall burn the weapons with fire." It is now reported that Russia is making weapons from a treated wood called lignostone. This is wood, which, when chemically treated is stronger than steel, yet remains elastic. The British are using a similar material for gears in their large vehicles. This material burns brilliantly, with intense heat. I have a friend who has built some of the toughest mountain highways in the world. He is a complete believer in the superiority of treated, laminated wood over steel for things like bridges, or even the frameworks of huge earth-moving machines.

Idealistic youth throughout the free world understandably protest: why this exorbitant annual expenditure of over 200 billion dollars on the insanity of making war, when 1½ million starve to death in Biafra? Over the last two years, altogether apart from the movement from East Pakistan into India, there has been another 10 percent increase in the number of world refugees, which stands at a new all-time high of 17,226,915. Over 3½ million of the world's population died last year from starvation, and 66 percent of the world's population goes hungry every day; 50 percent dies without ever having known a full stomach. Is this condition just? Of course not. Will it worsen? Yes. Jesus, who knew that only His second advent could cure this state of affairs, notified us that a "signal" for His "coming and the end of the age" would be "famines" in "different parts of the world." In Revelation 18 we read of some of the details of "famine" which is yet to strike. Think of the terrible starvation and famine in East Pakistan, famine which drives, as Prime Minister Gandhi laments, ten million of them over into an already starving India. Senator Edward Kennedy, visiting Pakistani refugee camps, refers to the situation as "the greatest human disaster of our time."

This is hard for North Americans to grasp. There have been recent news items indicating that the birth rates in both the U.S.A. and Canada are now the lowest in their respective histories, and yet with modern means of variety improvements, fertilization and irrigation, there is no end in sight as to the quantities of food surpluses which we seem capable of producing. It is currently estimated that with present farming methods, the world is capable of growing enough food to feed well, forty billion people; in short, ten times the population of today's world with enough and to spare. South America's agricultural lands alone could support nine billion.

The tragic truth is that the world is on the verge of mass starvation. In Cuba bread is the only food which is not stringently rationed. How could one who had been there ever forget the streets of Calcutta where a mother will chop the limbs off her infant as a means of soliciting sympathy and a few rupees from Westerners? By 1975, there will be four billion people and by 1986, five billion in our world. In the *Bangkok Post,* I read a review of the Englishmen William and Paul Paddock's *Famine, Nineteen Seventy-Five,* in which it is contended that it is now too late to avert mass famine in the Orient and Africa.

A seemingly insoluble problem for political science is how to utilize the world's labor force to produce the needed food to offset famine. One report reveals that in mid-1971 320 million — that is, one out of four — of the world's workers are unemployed. And the situation is getting worse rather than better.

The Stanford biologist, Paul Ehrlich, in headlining articles quoted throughout the world reckons that "there is not the slightest hope of escaping a disastrous time of famines from 1975 onward. It is shockingly apparent that the battle to feed man will end in a rout." A group of 172 eminent people from 19 countries, including 39 Nobel prize winners, and headed by Sir Julian Huxley, have petitioned the U.N. to halt the population explosion by any and every means. Unless drastic steps are taken, "there is in prospect a dark age of human misery, famine, and unrest which could generate growing panic, exploding into wars fought to appropriate the dwindling means of survival."

Professor L. C. Birch writes in *The Australian* that during the next half-dozen years, food production would have to be tripled to meet the nutritional demands of the world. It will be fortunate if it can be increased by 65 percent. In fact, there was no increase in the combined output of the world's farms and fisheries, while the population increased 2.7 percent. Of the additional billion people who are expected in the earth's population over the next decade, three-quarters will be added to the very poor countries, where annual incomes average one two-hundredth what they are in the United States and Canada. Columnist James Breslin asks: Is it right to spend 30 billion dollars to get a man on the moon, while children throughout the world have worms coming out of their mouths, and while countless others have so little going in? Is this right? It is another of the open-ended questions. According to the Scriptures, it is but another reason why our Lord must come again. Giving up the moon probes won't solve this crisis, but Christ's return will!

And when Jesus said there would be famines to signify His near return, He also said there would be "pestilences in divers places." This could refer relevantly to what the Russians call bacteriological warfare, or the Americans call biological warfare. Senator Robert Sikes of Florida warns that the Americans have a whole arsenal of biological weapons, one of which could kill one billion people. He goes on to estimate that the Russians have seven to eight times the capability of the United States in chemical biological warfare.

Or it could refer to the great disease ravages across the world. In Canada, with a population of only twenty million, we are told that due to the excesses of cigarette smoking, a million Canadians have lung cancer at some stage of development, and that unless some other disease gets in ahead, it will eventually kill every one of its victims. Each cigarette a heavy smoker lights cuts, on the average, fifteen minutes off his life. Ann Landers' column reckons that fifty million Americans, alive in 1971, will eventually capitulate to cancer unless a cure is found.

*The Australian* affirms that cigarette smokers are ten times more likely to die of lung cancer; six times more likely to die of bronchitis and emphysema; three times more likely to have a heart attack; much more likely to get cancer of the larynx, esophagus, and bladder; to have unsuccessful pregnancies; and to have such misfortunes as car accidents. On the average, smokers have one third more illnesses than non-smokers and live eight years less. But all the warnings throughout the world have little effect, for the annual increase of cigarettes sold continues at the rate of seventy billion more each year. And in mid-1971, it is officially announced that more Americans are smoking cigarettes than ever before. The tragic increase of drugs and narcotics addicts currently is at the rate of .7% per month.

Another pestilence is venereal disease. It has quadrupled in Canada. In California, by 1971, one in ten teen-agers allegedly had contracted it; in the central sections of big cities, as high as one in three. Throughout the world, it was seemingly checked in the post-war years by antibiotics, but they no longer can cope with it and it is now raging rampant in every country on earth — reaching "pandemic proportions."

In Australia, I was reading of another pestilence: Bubonic Plague, also known as the Black Death, because of its resemblance to the disease which killed one out of every four Europeans in the fourteenth century. It is currently getting a grip on the backward tribes of Vietnam, Laos, Cambodia and other Asian countries.

We thought we could abolish such diseases as cholera until the terrible outbreak in East Pakistan and India in 1971. *Time* magazine (June 21, 1971) actually uses the word "pestilence" to describe "this cholera epidemic that has barely begun, yet has already taken some 5,000 lives. It is almost a Biblical catalogue of woe, rivaling if not surpassing the plagues visited upon the Egyptians of Mosaic days." *Time* adds to the cholera epidemic the 500,000 East Pakistanis killed by the 1970 cyclone: another pestilence.

Perhaps the most frightening pestilence of our time, and certainly the most publicized, is pollution. One of the phenomena with which the 1970s were ushered in was the sudden attention the whole world — young and old, East and West — gave to this matter of pollution. Until the '70s few of us had ever heard the word ecology. Now most sixth-graders can tell you not only its meaning, but that before the century is out, the pollution of our whole physical environment will be such that the human race will be suffocated or poisoned to death. A responsible member of President Nixon's Cabinet has predicted that unless dramatic and universal anti-pollutant measures were adopted immediately, man would not survive the century. Early in 1971, *Christianity Today* carried an interview with an ecology expert who insisted that the suffocation of man by atmospheric, land, water and food pollutants was an inexorable threat demanding immediate remedy or sure doom. "Laugh In" pictured New Yorkers staring up through the street smog of 1976 and trying to identify what a dim midday light was; suddenly an old-timer calls on his memory to reckon that it could be the sun.

Into the hands of Americans in 1971 comes *Doomsday,* a thoroughly scholarly, if dull, 795-page book on man's collision course with death from pollution. As someone has suggested, ours is an "elegant technological society which underwent biological disintegration for a lack of ecological understanding." And so to the list of scientific and technological inventions for the potential annihilation of man is added extermination from over-powering pollution. But Jesus Christ will come again to cope with pollution.

The other signal of His coming and of the end of the age which our Lord put forward in that particular sentence was that there would be ". . . earthquakes in different parts of the world" (Matthew 24:7, Phillips). These would culminate, according to Revelation 18, in "a violent earthquake, like none before it in human history, so violent it was." A prominent historian of seismology, after nearly a lifetime of study, reckons that in the fourteenth century there were 137 major earthquakes; in the fifteenth century there were 174; in the sixteenth, 253; in the seventeenth, 2,119. The celebrated Harvard seismologist, Don Leet, observes that there are some 30 major earthquakes per year, with another 35 less serious ones. If these figures are accurate, that's up 2,189 percent in six centuries.

Newspapers recently have been carrying more and more frequent articles on the sharp increase in earthquakes. For example, in March, 1962, the first measurable earthquake in Colorado's history took place. During the following six years, there were 1,600.

*The Chicago Tribune* over a two-year period failed to report an earthquake somewhere in the world on only four days. A Presbyterian minister tells me that there are annually 18,000 earthquakes of a size large enough to be classified as such. An estimated 30,000 people lost their lives in Khorassan Province in Iran in the 1968 earthquake disaster. In

1970. in Peru. it was twice as many fatalities in what Robert Finch of the President's Cabinet called "the largest natural disaster in the modern history of the Western Americas." In 1971. it was Southern California and central Turkey.

*Time* points out that seismologists "repeatedly have warned that, because of the stress along the San Andreas fault" the State of California is overdue for a major catastrophe. A West Coast seismologist, Val Peterson, warns that after a careful computation of all the factors which will bring pressure on the crust of the earth over the next 50 years, there is certain to be a dramatic increase in earthquakes.

One of the best-attended movies in the San Francisco Bay area during the summer of 1971 is the Time-Life film produced by the British Broadcasting Corporation, a documentary entitled: "The City That Waits to Die." It endeavors to warn the people of that area that they are soon due for an earthquake which will kill 100,000 persons, perhaps many more. Says a concerned sponsor: "We keep piling up people on the most dangerous fault on the planet."

Frightening as the San Andreas fault may be. there is no assurance as far as Biblical prophecy is concerned that such a formidable disaster will necessarily occur. But according to Zechariah 14 even "the earthquake in the days of Uzziah" will be dwarfed by the one which will occur when the "day of the Lord cometh." At that time the Mount of Olives will "cleave in the midst thereof toward the east and toward the west, and there shall be a very great valley; and half of the mountain shall remove toward the north, and half of it toward the south." Seismologists have discovered a major fault and therefore an earthquake-prone line here which coincides with the Biblical prophecy of Old Testament times. On this basis several hotel and inn chains have flatly rejected proposals to build in this area.

When God ordains the earth to be shaken by the powers of nature, Jesus said that it is just another signal that He is coming soon. When the 60 people were killed in the Los Angeles area earthquake in 1971, it seemed as though all the media wondered if it was an ordained act of God signaling a Divine advent of some kind.

Many people ask: "Is there an intimation of television in the Bible?" I do not know. But for centuries and perhaps especially since such books as Professor Urey's (the Nobel Prize winner) *The Red Lights of the Apocalypse* appeared, fascination has centered on Revelation 11. We read that "when they (the two witnesses) have completed their testimony" and have been killed "their corpses will lie in the street of the great city" where "also their Lord was crucified. For three days and a half men from . . . every language and nation, gaze upon [them]." Indeed, "all men on earth gloat over them" (7-9, NEB). This statement seemed bizarre and ludicrous until made possible by television with the help of space satellites such as Telstar and Early Bird pioneered. An estimated one billion transfixed people, at one time, watched with bated breath as Neil Armstrong set foot on the moon.

As a posture in the midst of all these signs in science and technology which are indicative of a sure and imminent hope, Jesus instructed His followers that they could expect to "see the Son of Man coming in a cloud with great power and splendor! But when these things begin to happen, look up, hold your heads high, for you will soon be free!" (Luke 21:27, Phillips).

In the light of the foregoing, was it in vain that President Richard Nixon should have laid his hand on a passage of Scripture recorded in Isaiah 2 as he delivered his Inauguration address? Indeed not! For when Christ comes again, to usher in His Kingdom, men will indeed say to one another, in the words of that passage, "Come ye, and let us go up to the mountain of the Lord . . . and he will teach us of his ways, and we will walk in his paths . . . and he shall judge among the nations . . . and they shall beat their swords into plowshares, and their spears into pruninghooks: nation shall not lift up sword against nation, neither shall they learn war any more" (Isaiah 2:3, 4). Eric Sevareid, the CBS analyst, is right, amidst the writhings of 1971, to aspire for "the dawn of a new era" when "lions may lie down peacefully with lambs as the prophets foretold."

Nor is the longing of our youth for peace and justice in vain. When St. Peter told of how the heavens and the earth would be ravaged with what would seem to resemble very closely a thermonuclear destruction, he promised that believers in Christ should not give up, but look up: "True, this day will mean that the . . . elements disintegrate in fearful heat, but our hopes are set not on these but on . . . the new earth which He has promised us, and in which nothing but good shall live."

Man, on his own, cannot produce the "New World Comin'!" for which the pop lyricist craves. The tools man is increasingly developing, but not the character! His inveterate disposition, as Eric Hoffer puts it, destroys his dream: "Everywhere we look at present we see something new trying to be born. A pregnant, swollen world is writhing in labor, and everywhere untrained quacks are officiating as obstetricians. These quacks say that the only way the new era can be born is by a Caesarean operation. They lust to rip the belly of the world open." The coming again of Jesus Christ is the great therapy of eternity breaking in upon wounded time.

Chancellor Solandt of the University of Toronto

craves that the money spent on armaments be spent on peace and provision for prosperity. When Christ comes, it will. I believe that no invention of science and technology will be lost or used for any destructive device at that time. In the favorite words (first written by Moses) of one of America's greatest native-born philosophers, revivalist and Princeton president Jonathan Edwards, "but as truly as I live, all the earth shall be filled with the glory of the Lord." As Milton put it, "At return of Him, thy Saviour and Lord; In glory of the Father . . . New earth . . . founded in righteousness, peace and love; To bring forth fruits, joy and eternal bliss."

# Chapter Three

# Society and the Coming Christ

On every hand, writers are stating that society has gone sour and civilization is sick. Writing on the current sickness in society, Harold Lindsell, editor-in-chief of *Christianity Today,* points out that "this present world is doomed. The scent of death is upon it. It is commiting suicide and nothing can save it . . . until the coming of Jesus Christ." Attorney General John Mitchell says that the America of 1971 clearly is "more imperiled from within than from without." Prime Minister Pierre Trudeau comments that his greatest fear for Canada is a complete social breakdown of society from within. Mayor John Lindsay of New York, confronted with a megalopolis whose social monstrosities hang him on the horns of a thousand dilemmas, turns in mid-1971 to the Church and implores help. As the Metro-Mayor of Toronto, William Allen, a devout Catholic, speaks of society breaking down and the people we look to for help — clergymen, politicians and professors — adopting attitudes of irresponsibility at the very time their interventions for good are most needed. Pope Paul VI laments that we are victims of a "world in the throes of unprecedented change"; that "everyone has the impression of being dragged away and overcome

59

by an irresistible current . . . seized by frenzy." He laments that our "youth virtually rejoices in the disorder that it provokes and the problems it arouses."

This, the Bible forecasts, would be something of the state of society at the time of Christ's second coming: a maelstrom of lawlessness; a hurricane of violence; a tornado of selfishness; a cyclone of sexual incontinence; a typhoon of revolt against the tried, traditional structures of society. Upheaval and chaos would threaten order and serenity of any kind. In the words of a new film, "Sex, Hate and Violence" are in the saddle. Sir Cyril Black, the distinguished British M.P., pleads that all law-abiding citizens combine to "slam on the brakes on a sick society." A good idea? Yes. Can we? It seems not. Hell-bent man has gone beyond the point of no return. Only the return of Jesus Christ can stem the current moral and social landslide.

New Testament writers predicted that lawlessness would prevail at the time of Christ's coming: such anarchy as would make sane people cry out for law and order, a law and order which only Christ Himself could institute and maintain. Surely St. Paul must have felt at times that Roman rule was cruel and often difficult to accept, but he wrote to the Romans, "Every person must submit to the supreme authorities. There is no authority but by act of God, and the existing authorities are instituted by him; consequently anyone who rebels against authority is resisting a divine institution, and those who so resist have themselves to thank for the punishment they will receive. For government, a terror to crime, has no terrors for good behaviour" (Romans 13:1-3, NEB).

St. Peter made it very plain that prior to the day of Judgment there will be ". . . those who have indulged all the foulness of their lower natures, and have nothing but contempt for authority . . . These

men, with no more sense than the unreasoning brute
beasts ... delight in daylight self-indulgence; ...
and with their high-sounding nonsense they use the
sensual pull of the lower passions to attract those
who were just on the point of cutting loose from
their companions in misconduct" (2 Peter 2:10, 12,
13, 18, Phillips). This, it seems to me, is a precise
description of brash young North Americans, who
will take the flag of the nation which has given them
birth and the highest standard of living in history
and burn it in open defiance and contempt. "Youth,"
laments Pope Paul VI, "virtually rejoices in the disorder that it provokes and the problems it arouses."

Crime in the United States has gone up 119 percent during the last decade, increasing 9 times as
fast as the population growth. The Attorney General
has announced that major crime in the United States
in 1971 has jumped another 6 percent over 1970.
And the F.B.I. reports that violent crime in cities of
more than one million has increased 21 percent over
the same period. President Nixon reckons that organized crime is doing a 45 billion dollar "take" annually on the American people. As crime is escalated
by the presence of a third of a million heroin addicts
a U.S. senator believes that what is ahead for America will make the crime syndicates of the 1920's
look like a Sunday school picnic in comparison. In
Britain, crime has doubled during the last decade,
and, according to a newspaper article, juvenile crime
arrests in France have gone up 900 percent during
the same period. And from West Germany in mid-
1971 comes the news that crime there is escalating,
some crimes having more than doubled since the
late sixties.

Avery Brundage, President of the International
Olympic Committee, laments that "the rebellion of
youth today is worldwide." Every responsible citizen

of a free society is concerned. Former President Johnson sees "a nation of captives, imprisoned nightly behind chained doors, double locks and barred windows." On national television he exhorted, "For God's sake resolve to live under the law." Ninety percent of the Americans polled as to what they consider to be the biggest issue in the land today replied, "law and order." In mid-1971 a task force of the President's Commission on Violence reports that the United States is moving toward "the modern counterpart of the fortified Medieval city." A Chief of Police in Ontario says that the whole communications media: radio, television, newspapers and magazines seem wittingly or unwittingly to be aligned against law enforcement officers: "Our image is being destroyed." U.S. citizens are reacting to all of this with both defensive and offensive preparation. The burglar alarm business has gone up 600 percent in the last five years, an annual billion dollars now being poured into these defensive mechanisms. A national magazine claims that in mid-1971, there are 200 million rifles in the U.S.A.

Law enforcement agencies are being beefed up, and reorganized. Their non-lethal weaponry expenditure in the United States was doubled back in 1968 over 1967, and by 1972 is to be up 1,200 percent over 1967. But can they stem the tidal wave? Even the young are concerned. "What is this world coming to?" writes a teen-ager to Ann Landers, "It seems the only place one is safe anymore, is in his grave."

Paul and Peter, while writing of the conditions which would prevail throughout the world at the time of Christ's coming, might specifically have had Israel in mind, since they were both Jews. Crime in Israel, according to *Time* (June 21, 1971), "is soaring to levels that upright Israel has never known.

In greater Tel Aviv (pop. 800,000), robberies are up 125% since last year, murders have doubled, purse snatchers have become common and 400 prostitutes are on the street." The true Christian should not give up on social action. He is not looking for an excavation in the cemetery in which to bury a degenerated society, but elevation to the skies, and with this expectation he can strive for reform in a deteriorating society, without capitulating to despair.

What has now begun to typify lawless acts is violence, yet another sure sign that the Prince of Peace must come again. "The earth also was corrupt before God, and the earth was filled with violence," was Moses' description of social conditions in Noah's day. "And God said unto Noah, the end of all flesh is come before me; for the earth is filled with violence. . ." (Genesis 6:11, 13). Declared our Lord, "As things were in Noah's days, so will they be when the Son of Man comes."

"Violence — physical violence, physical intimidation," says President Nixon, "is seemingly on its way to becoming an accepted form of opinion-forming in today's world." So conservative an organ as *The Wall Street Journal* reckons human "society is sick and frighteningly violent." "The instinct for violence," sighs Arthur Schlesinger, Jr., "is almost as if a primal curse has been fixed on our nation. We are a violent people." "Savage violence," says Governor Hughes of New Jersey, "is running through our society." "Violence . . . terrorism and reprisal," laments Pope Paul, "send a painful quiver through the entire body of mankind." Prime Minister Trudeau sums up one of his years in office with the characterization, "A year of violence and destruction." Neither British football or Pakistani soccer matches are any longer free from rashes of violence where rampaging fans, fanned into a rage by the slightest provocation, will leave a trail of wrecked trains and broken bones in their wake. William Davis, Premier of Ontario, finds intolerable the "hooliganism by those who try to destroy our universities." Mild and orderly protests seem to be a thing of the past. Non-violence is passé. At Cornell University 110 under-grads march out of the student center brandishing 17 rifles and shotguns with which they bring the administration to its knees.

The British film censor John Trevelyan resigned in mid-1971 because he protests that in Britain, where there has traditionally been comparative calm and justice, films are now going over to violence of the most hideous and revolting stamp.

In California, the *Los Angeles Times* claims that at least three of the baseball Angels are "carrying guns and several others are known to have hidden knives to use as protection in case of fights among themselves." Says the American League's champion-ship batter: "Going to hell would even be an im-provement," to continuing with the "Angels."

What is it that produces this wave of violence across our world: mob violence and vicious loners like Lee Harvey Oswald, Richard Speck and Charles Whitman? Man in the 1970s is caught in "the sardine syndrome," as the English social biologist, Dr. Wil-liam Russell points out, adding "every time man enters a population crisis, the period is marked by very acute social tensions which lead to extensive, unrestrained violence." "Our boring lives lead to violence," reckons psychologist Erich Fromm. *Look* magazine points to television, claiming that in one major American city, TV stations showed 7,887 acts of violence in one week. It seems to me that the sudden rash of guilt which got Hollywood stars to confess their culpability before national press clubs and television audiences when Martin Luther King, Jr., and Robert Kennedy were shot, was not far off the mark. Such movies as "Bonnie and Clyde," "Pretty Poison," "In Cold Blood," "In the Heat of the Night," and "A Minute to Pray; A Second to Die!" incite violence. Even worse are their 1971 successors: "Bloody Mama," "The Last Run," and "Bunny O'Hane." So do the social injustices which callously leave jammed in steaming ghettos people who see no other hope than to explode in violence. As the President's Commission points out, city crowding and exposing youth to live war scenes from Vietnam and, what is worse, the clever but sinister portrayal of human hate, sadism and cruelty which pour forth from the pens of playwrights whose minds are grotesquely depraved and twisted, contribute to the problem.

That there are professional riot planners whose design it is to undermine and overthrow our democratic way of life, leaders like Wilson, De Gaulle, Diefenbaker, Johnson and Nixon have all repeatedly pointed out, and about this there can be no doubt. The pouring of outside money into the Washington marches of 1971 gave evidence of this. Whither violence? Robert Ardrey, in his play, *The Territorial Imperative,* comprehensively explores man's chances of escaping a nuclear holocaust. He puts hope at a pretty low ebb when he concludes that as long as you can crowd "viciously snarling animals" and a high degree of sophistication into the same people and push them into places of determinative decision, you don't leave much room for the survival concept. Violence has climbed into the saddle and savagery threatens from various strata the survival of society in its present form. The *Rangley* (Colorado) *Times* observes that "After several thousand years, civilization has advanced to the point where we bolt all our doors and windows at night, while the jungle natives sleep in an open hut." "Even the churches now encourage violence," laments *Time* magazine.

What is it that has gone wrong with man? St. Paul wrote to Timothy that "God's Spirit specifically tells us that in later days there will be men . . . whose consciences are as dead as seared flesh" (1 Timothy 4:1, 2, Phillips). To quote Robert Ardrey again, "Man is by inerasable nature as aggressive as an animal." In Toronto on Hallowe'en, a hundred cases were cited of razor blades and needles being put into oranges and apples, and handed out in response to little children's voices, "Tricks or treats." It is these sick acts, all the way up to thermonuclear warmongering, which make such responsible people as Senator Dodd of Connecticut say, "Our society is going crazy," or Senator Jackson of Washington bemoan, "The world has gone mad." One of our most famous Torontonians, Marshall McLuhan, forecasts that the whole mentality of the rising generation is being brainwashed by television, and no one really knows where this road is taking us. By the time a youth graduates from high school, he has, on the average, seen 15,000 hours of television. Add to this the psychedelic drugs which are doubling annually the number of addicts, along with the recent wave of mainlining in which heroin is taking over from marijuana, and one begins to realize just how rifled through our society is becoming with fiendish men whose "conscience is branded with the devil's sign."

Possibly it is just this factor of man being so incognito, living in limbo, and flung into the rat race of life which militates toward his becoming so selfish and egocentric. Is this not precisely as St. Paul predicted? "In the last days the times will be full of danger. Men will become utterly self-centered . . . loving all the time what gives them pleasure . . ."

(2 Timothy 3:1, 2, 4, Phillips). ". . . There will come in the last days mockers who live according to their own godless desires. . . . men who complain and curse their fate while trying all the time to mold life according to their own desires. They 'talk big' but will pay men great respect if it is to their own advantage" (Jude 18, 16, Phillips). Witness the "great respect" given to a Che Guevara, a Herbert Marcuse or a Jerry Rubin.

Lionel Rubinoff, the York University philosopher, has published a most fascinating book, *The Pornography of Power*. In it he makes none of the now exploded behavioristic, altruistic claims as to man's innate goodness. In lieu, he says frankly that man must face the evil of his own heart. Only instead of prescribing a cure, he suggests that man capitulate by giving full imaginative expression to the whole gamut of his evil proclivities — hedonism, the ancient Greeks called it. Max Lerner concludes that "America is now living a Babylonian existence." An Australian legislator pays a visit to Britain and returns completely disillusioned, commenting, "England is lost in a sargasso sea of sex, sadism, and psychedelics." And CBS advertises the showing of the film, "The World, the Flesh, and the Devil," assuring viewers that it will "really turn you on," as if getting oneself turned on is the chief end of living. The Puritans were a happy people because they attempted to live by the rule: for every look you take at yourself, take ten at Christ. Too often today, God hardly rates a glance.

The projection of selfishness is covetousness. The apostles Peter, Paul, Jude, James and John all predicted that greed would be a characteristic of the times immediately preceding the return of Christ. "In their greed for money they will trade on your credulity with sheer fabrications," forecast St. Peter, adding that they will be "... past masters in mercenary greed" (2 Peter 2:3, 14, NEB). Before the Lord comes, indicated St. Jude, some men would stoop to follow "... error for pay" (Jude 11, NEB). "In an age that is near its close," projected St. James, certain men will "... have piled up wealth" (James 5:3, NEB). Uncaring and unsparing in their exploitations, James charged, "The wages you never paid to the men who mowed your fields are loud against you, and the outcry of the reapers has reached the ears of the Lord of Hosts. You have lived on earth in wanton luxury, fattening yourselves like cattle — and the day for slaughter has come. You have condemned the innocent and murdered him; he offers no resistance ... To you who have great possessions: weep and wail over the miserable fate descending on you. Your riches have rotted; your fine clothes are moth-eaten; your silver and gold have rusted away, and their very rust will be evidence against you and consume your flesh like fire ..." (James 5:4-6, 1-3, NEB).

St. John predicted in his Revelation of Jesus Christ of how the smug rich would boast, "I am rich, I have prospered, and there is nothing that I need," not knowing that you are "pitiable" and "poverty-stricken" (Revelation 3:17, Phillips). The mad pursuit of materialism can be seen in best sellers like Adam Smith's *The Money Game,* Lundberg's *The Rich and the Super Rich,* Cameron Hawley's *Executive Suite,* Morton Shulman's *Anyone Can Make a Million,* and Louis Auchincloss' *The Guilty Ones.* These deify the glories of being rich. The fact that a hundred millionaires commit suicide each year in the United States gives evidence of the fact that money in itself is not a passport to happiness. The message seems to get through to very few.

The press featured a film actress as "the world's most successful woman" who earns $1,250,000 per film plus 10 percent of the profits, plus $50,000 a week overtime, plus travel expenses. At 40 she has been married five times, currently owns three Rolls Royces, a yacht, many of the world's most valuable and fabulous jewels and paintings. "Yet there is about this lovely creature an inevitable sadness, a prescience of doom, the feeling that inevitably life is passing her by." The American woman spends two billion dollars per year on beauty aids. Yet, during the last year there is a 67 percent increase among her sex who commit suicide and a 43 percent increase in alcoholism. Who knows how many took to drugs? Can riches procure happiness for the fairer sex? Obviously not!

As for the Communist world, their whole way of life is built on the blandishly materialist theory that "a man is what he eats." There has never in history been a political philosophy so undisguisedly based on sheer materialism as that of Marxism, and as Winston Churchill said, "Everyone can see how Communism rots the soul of a nation, how it makes it hungry and abject indeed, and proves a base and abominable reward." Unmistakably, it is feeding, clothing, and housing Red China just above the base line. But it robs its people's souls. They are sealed in a system of total spiritual ignorance. For those of us who have an abundance of material things, Jesus warned of a spate of overeating and drunkenness which would spread over the world. "In the time of the coming of the Son of Man, life will be as it was in the days of Noah," apprised Jesus, when "people ate and drank" (Luke 17:26, 27, Phillips). That would constitute the existence of multitudes: their contrived *raison d'être*. "Keep a watch on yourselves," our Lord later forewarned those who at that time would be His followers; "do not let your minds be dulled by dissipation and drunkenness and worldly cares so that the great Day closes upon you suddenly like a trap" (Luke 21:34, NEB). Gluttony, according to the American Medical Association, is currently a foremost hazard to good health in the United States. We have already mentioned famine as a sign of Christ's coming again. It struck me, as I walked down the streets of Calcutta, that here were tens of millions of people in India trying desperately to get started eating. In North America, tens of millions are trying to get stopped.

And there would be drunkenness. Eighty percent of Canadian adults consume liquor, leaving a trail of a quarter of a million alcoholics. A leading physician concludes that alcohol is now North America's third greatest killer, behind heart disease and cancer. According to WLS radio, 61 percent of the fatal automobile accidents in the United States are caused by liquor. In France, it is 66 percent. In 1971, Italy becomes "the world's No. 1 alcohol consumers." *Look* magazine claims that 5½ million Americans are alcoholics and the cost of liquor to employers through absenteeism and inefficiency is a staggering bill. Tom Skinner asserts that for every American drug addict there are 300 alcoholics. No parent earns the right to tell his child to get off drugs if he gets drunk. It is reported that in 1971 90 percent of the British are drinkers and that the consumption of alcoholic beverages in Japan is up 10 percent over 1970.

Ann Landers' column describes the torment inflicted on a home by a drunken father: "People who live with the screaming, beating, broken glass, black eyes, knocked-out teeth, police at the door, bill collectors, the whole ugly bit," are aware that there is a price which goes with alcoholism. An editor of

*McLean's* writes that men traditionally have been alcoholics because, like the Englishman who got drunk every weekend, it is "the shortest route out of Manchester." Today, many in responsible posts in our world are drunken because they adopt the attitude that the world is going to blow up one way or another anyway, and intoxication is a temporary escape. But instead of helping people retain their sanity, alcoholism brings insanity on. The Ann Landers' column indicates that one American in four suffers from some form of mental imbalance. Forty percent of the Frenchmen in mental institutions are alcoholics. Here again is where Christ's coming again is so practical. It gives hope and assurance that ultimately our Lord is coming again to institute a redeemed society.

Undoubtedly sex is the social area where degeneration morally shows up most sharply. "In the last days," wrote St. Paul, people will be "incontinent," "intemperate," "utterly lacking in purity," while "seducers shall wax worse and worse." Jesus portended that pressure would be brought to bear ". . . to seduce, if it were possible, even the elect. But take ye heed: behold, I have foretold you all things" (Mark 13:22, 23). St. Peter presaged how men in society would ". . . make of sensual lusts and debauchery a bait to catch those who have barely begun to escape from their heathen environment. They promise them freedom, but are themselves slaves of corruption; for a man is the slave of whatever has mastered him" (2 Peter 2:18, 19, NEB). The whole swing of public communications is toward what the protagonists of sexually permissive and completely promiscuous attitude toward life call "the open society." In the words of a *Time* cover story, ours is the era of "The Sex Explosion." So *Playboy* becomes the most read, or, should we say, gazed at, magazine in the world, its circulation in its few years of existence already soaring to six million.

A school principal tells me that in one of the new community colleges in Ontario, in the literature department, *Playboy* has become the official textbook! I had never before heard of any magazine being the textbook for any class in any academic institution, at any level of learning, anywhere in the world, but *Playboy* has done it!

There are twenty million magazines per week, sold in the United States, in an annual waste of a billion dollars undisguisedly purporting to purvey nothing but sex. Such themes as "I took my daughter's place in her husband's arms," are strewn over the covers.

Leonard Cohen of McGill, and John Updike of Harvard, join the ranks of the world's best-known writers by exploiting sex to the hilt. The latter's *Couples* heads the best-seller lists for months at a time then moves over to make room for *Everything You Always Wanted to Know About Sex*. Lyle Stuart is laughing all the way to the bank with the proceeds of *The Sensuous Woman, The Sensuous Man,* and *Naked Came the Stranger,* candidly admitting that a few years ago "we would have all gone to jail." Films and stage plays such as "The Orgy Girls," "The Game is Sex," "I Am Curious — Yellow," "I a Woman," "Oh! Calcutta!" "What Do You Say to a Naked Lady?" and "Relations" (from Denmark!), make "Some Like It Hot" with Marilyn Monroe look as if the latter was acted under the supervision of a Victorian prude. Kenneth Tynan deliberately wrote "Oh! Calcutta!" as a sensual "stimulation, where a fellow can take a girl he is trying to woo!" According to *Newsweek,* sex relations made it on stage for the first time in April, 1969, with "Che!" — a Broadway play which features among other things, an ape raping a nun.

Students are called upon to read what a Prime Minister calls "ostentatious obscenity in university newspapers." Truth is often something which is supposed to be between the lines.

"Sex-wise," sums up a leading Metropolitan editorial, this "was a pretty big year . . . It was the first time couples began popping up in magazines . . . announcing proudly that they were living together in what we used to call sin." It is a fact that men are more and more as they were in Noah's day, as Jesus predicted they would be, when "God saw that the wickedness of man was great in the earth, and that every imagination of the thoughts of his heart was only evil continually" (Genesis 6:5). Lord Elton of Oxford claims that something like 83 percent of the modern novel centers in perverting Judeo-Christian moral laws. Is it any wonder that Jude forecast: "Their dreams lead them to defile"? Jude linked dreams and sexual promiscuity long before that other Jewish seer, Sigmund Freud, appeared on the scene. An English educator once said to me that however sophisticated much modern writing is, one would think that those who produced much of it were living in a sewer. "Since Yvonne De Gaulle passed from the scene," notes *Newsweek,* "nearly all sexual restraints have passed from the 'Gay Paree' scene." *Time* tells us of sex emporiums being built "to view the copulation" — live and in color — as next in the sexists' plans for the future. It also describes how a few blocks from Times Square "couples cavort in the nude and simulate intercourse" while cameramen are shooting round the clock. Add to this the TV cassettes which will soon bring any variety of sex films in color into homes around the world.

Obsession with sex leads to a recrudescence of nudity. St. John could well have been writing of this when he indicated, ". . . you have no eyes to see that you are . . . naked" (Revelation 3:17, Phillips). St. Peter indicated that men's eyes would indeed be occupied, however, as he foresaw swingers ". . . reveling in their dissipation, carousing with you. They have eyes full of adultery, insatiable for sin" (2 Peter 2:13, 14, RSV). Nudist camps date back to 1912 in Germany, but only in the last few years have they become widespread. There are now 350,000 nudists in the United States, according to the secretary of the American Sunbathing Association. (This, of course, is exclusive of the kids who go nude when they feel like it.) Nakedness on a mass scale, not just in nudist colonies and burlesque shows, however, is the latest craze of the purveyors of sexual permissiveness.

Sydney Katz, the columnist, foresees the society of the future in which females will wear nothing but a bit of translucent paint to accentuate their features, with a heavy spray of transparent foam over their bodies to insulate them from the discomforts which weather conditions impose, but not from the voluptuous gaze of depraved males. The British film censor, John Trevelyan, rationalizes that nudity is inevitable, but that the public needs some conditioning for the full frontal nude.

Since British stage censorship ended recently there has been a rash of plays on nudity such as "Hair," "Man's Eyes," "The Beard," and "Canada's Fortune." A girl strips naked in the stately Albert Hall and elicits from Sir Cyril Black in lamentation that Britain now is indeed a "sick society."

But the pro-voices are louder than the cons, these days. Even John Lennon, his Japanese wife and Paul McCartney appear in the nude on the cover of a Beatle record: as if we hadn't seen enough of the Beatles already! Richard Harris stars in a Western, riding naked like his horse in a "raving sexcess."

It seems ironic that in Nairobi, Kenya, the Minister of Education has to appeal to American teachers who come to Kenya in connection with the Peace Corps to refrain from wearing miniskirts and other sparse dress. After all, it was Anglo-Americans (he meant, of course, the Christian missionaries), who had taught the Africans the virtues of concealing nakedness and now he hoped they would not come out and undo the good which they had done in generations past.

This inordinate pre-occupation with sex leads to gross and shameless immorality, both pre-marital and extra-marital, its proportions today a sign that Christ must come back and right this wrong. St. Paul anticipated that in the final age of this world promiscuity would reach unprecedented proportions with "passionate and unprincipled" people who would "worm their way into people's houses, and find easy prey in silly women with an exaggerated sense of sin and morbid cravings" (2 Timothy 3:3, 6, 7, Phillips). Jesus forewarned that as in Noah's day along with their "eating and drinking," people would be "marrying and giving in marriage" (Matthew 24:38), the implication being that they will focus on marriage after marriage to the extent that they ignore spiritual and moral laws. In the Revelation of Jesus Christ, St. John forecast that a whole society would so engage in "fornication" that ". . . her sins are piled high as heaven" (Revelation 18:5, NEB).

*Reader's Digest* claims that 98 percent of Swedes engage in pre-marital intercourse and the average man over 30 years of age has or has had 7 sex partners; already the average for those between 18 and 30 is 8. A reporter from Russia writes in the *New Zealand Herald* that nearly all Russians have pre-marital relations. The average city girl in Russia has had several abortions before marriage, these being legal and free. And the divorce rate in Russia, according to the United Nations, is 26 percent higher than in the United States. Some months ago, *Newsweek* assessed that American morals had dipped more in the last year than in the previous fifty years and when *Time's* cover story was "The Adulterous Generation," one did not have to read far to realize how fast the skid downward is moving. In a recent year in Britain, there was an 8 percent increase in the number of divorces granted.

In 1870, there were 10,000 divorces in the United States. In 1970, there were 600,000. Add to this a million abortions. Tops of the pops like, "Have you Got Cheating on Your Mind," "Second Time Around," "Strangers in the Night," and the Rolling Stones' "Let's Spend the Night Together" are deliberately written and sung to promote immorality. As Billy Graham said in the Chicago crusade of 1971, there seem to be so few real love songs being written any more — just sex songs. With romance replaced by a rampaging sex mania, Dr. Wardell Pomeroy, past President of the American Association of Marriage and Family Counselors, sees group sex and wife-swapping in 1971 surging to the fore as a "phenomenon" all over the country.

The moral depravity which the Scriptures indicate God hates most is sexual deviation and perversion, including homosexuality and lesbianism. St. Jude (and St. Peter) foresaw that there would exist a society which paralleled that of Sodom and Gomorrah in this respect. These were the sins of those ancient twin-cities of iniquity. Before "the Lord cometh" wrote St. Jude, society would sink to the level of "Sodom and Gomorrah and the adjacent cities who . . . gave themselves up to sexual immorality and perversion" (Jude 7, Phillips). Whole novels and films are today centering on the theme of homosexuality. Richard Burton tells how repugnant it is for him and Rex Harrison to play the roles of homosexuals, but it is the way to make a quick buck. Hence, it is the theme of stage plays like "The Boys in the Band" (in London, nine homosexuals star). The title of an article in *The National Enquirer* is "The New People: desexualization in American Life." The big fad in clothes at the moment is "unisex." In London some Continental visitors kept entering the wrong washroom in a public institution because they were not able to read English well enough to distinguish "Men" from "Women" and the pictures on the respective doors were virtually identical. Complains a country western song: "I can't tell the Boys from the Girls."

Does this have its impact on practice? Yes. A physician was quoted in the *Toronto Star* a few months ago as assessing that there are 90,000 homosexuals in Metro-Toronto. A radio newscast announces that of Holland's population of 13 million, 5 percent are homosexuals. If Toronto and Holland have 5 percent homosexuality, it is probably a fair estimate to state that 5 percent of Europeans and North Americans are homosexual. God who created man "male and female" needs to come back and sort out His creation, and He has promised that He will.

More and more, sexual perversion is on the increase. *Reader's Digest* asserts that increasing numbers of books are making no reference whatsoever to natural sex relations. In place of normal heterosexual activity, there are sex-incited flagellations, sex deviation, men torture women, sadism, masochisms; men ask women to beat them; men kill women in sex crimes: every conceivable form of sexual deviation and perversion, which the most depraved imaginations can concoct.

All of this militates against marriage, of course. Is it any wonder then, that St. Paul foresees that as "God's Spirit specifically tells us . . ." there will be those who "forbid marriage" (1 Timothy 4:1, 3, Phillips)? Youth gods Mick Jagger of the Rolling Stones and John Lennon of the Beatles have gone on record to state, "Legal marriage, as such, is now obsolete." The result is that Jagger's "girl friend," Miss Faithful, is so depressed with an insecure relationship like this that in Sydney, Australia, she tries to commit suicide with barbiturates. A national magazine in the United States advertises a celebrity whose vaunted opinion is, "I'd rather be Dead than Wed."

The casting to the winds of the moral law of God means that children refuse to heed their parents. In an increasingly large number of instances they either don't know who their parents are, or are not brought up by them at all. Is it surprising then, that St. Paul foretold "the last days," in which children would be "disobedient to their parents" (2 Timothy 3:1, 2, RSV)? Jesus forewarned His disciples who wanted to know when He would return, that one of the phenomena would be that "Children will turn against their parents" (Matthew 10:21, NEB).

When I was in Africa, I read in a newspaper of a London school in which 5-to-7-year-olds were so completely out of hand that a Member of Parliament, John Silkin, reports "The problem is so serious that the staff are leaving through fear of mental and physical breakdown." Razor blade slashings and hangings were reported. "We have been told of open rebellion in the classroom. Children use the foulest language."

John Humphrey, the Canadian who serves as President of the United Nations Commission for Human Rights, points to the fact that the clash between the young who are in revolt and their parents, who form the adults of this generation, is so acute that unless this generation gap can be resolved, there is no hope for future society. It is alarming indeed to read that 75 percent of the school teachers of East St. Louis, Illinois, are armed. A public school principal tells me that the discipline problem in Ontario schools is completely out of hand in many places.

This generation gap is where Mr. Trudeau says our most critical problem lies, and this was the gap Senator Robert Kennedy was trying to bridge. I met Mr. Kennedy twelve days before his assassination, and I remember one of the Oregonites asking him why he had such long hair. He replied that it was to bridge the generation gap. *Life* magazine in analyzing the similarities of Mr. Kennedy's accused assassin, Sirhan Sirhan with Lee Harvey Oswald and James Earl Ray noted that all three came from broken homes. A West coast judge has stated that he would like to write a book on "I Hate Parents!" He is convinced that the reason for juvenile delinquency is parental profligacy.

With society in such a critical state, why are the majority not aware of their peril, and why do they not repent? Because, as St. Paul foresaw, "In the last days . . . men shall be . . . despisers of those that are good" (2 Timothy 3:3). We may be amazed by the fact that when an Ontario university opened, the freshmen were initiated by the sophomores, who led them up and down the corridors (allegedly of both the dormitories and the academic halls) shouting "Jesus Christ" several times over, and this was followed by an unrepeatable chain of expletives and four-letter words. Why does this happen? Because the "outlook of the lower nature is enmity with God; it is not subject to the law of God" (Romans 8:7,

NEB). What has to happen is that individuals in society be born again. Bishop Fulton Sheen is so right when he prescribes the foremost need of North Americans as being that they obey Jesus' remedy for human depravity, "You must be born again" (John 3:3, Phillips). Will society be born again? Can man not redeem it? The answer to the latter question is, "No," a fact of our times. The answer to the former, thank God, is, "Yes." When Jesus Christ comes again, He will ultimately redeem society. Today He is redeeming individuals in it.

# Chapter Four

# Philosophy and the Coming Christ

When Prime Minister Trudeau remarked on national television recently that "most of our problems are in our minds," he was simply reflecting the maxim cf the ancient Solomon who reasoned that "As [a man] thinketh . . . so is he" (Proverbs 23:7). We're not always what we think we are, but what we think: we are! Thinking does not simply get us out of binds, but as Mr. Trudeau implies, it gets us in. That's where man is today. Francis Bacon, who once argued that "All good moral philosophy is but the handmaid to religion," also cautioned that "A little philosophy inclineth man's mind to atheism; but depth in philosophy bringeth men's minds about to religion." St. Paul, himself a great philosopher, and completely at home reasoning the Gospel with philosophers as he did with the Athenian Stoics and Epicureans, exhorted the Colossians to "See to it that no one makes a prey of you by philosophy and empty deceit, according to human tradition" (Colossians 2:8, RSV). In lieu, "Set your minds on things that are above, not on things that are on earth." For "when Christ who is our life appears, then you also will appear with him in glory" (Colossians 3:2, 4, RSV). In short, anticipation of Christ's coming again is the best intellectual stimulant that a people can have; not mere mental activity, but positive thinking. It imparts hope.

The most read philosophers of our time are not optimists. The late English philosopher, Bertrand Russell, counseled that "The best we can hope for is unyielding despair." Possibly the best known philosopher of our time is the French existentialist, Jean Paul Sartre, an atheist (his more recent admissions that life has purpose betray second thoughts on whether or not there is not a God after all; yet he prefers to be known as an atheist). Sartre reasons that life is despair and death, his attitude to existence having been expressed in the title to his play, "No Exit."

One of the best books in this area is Alvin Toffler's *Future Shock*. He gives man almost no chance of surviving his own complete dehumanization through technological and demographical impingement. His best-seller decries the inexorable march of machine against man.

This aura of doom was in sharp evidence on a recent CBS television program featuring Jack Kroll, the senior editor of *Newsweek,* interviewing avantgarde playwrights Susan Sontag and Agnes Varda. Showing some "way out" filmstrips the conversation focused on the dominant ideas of the new films. There was unanimous concurrence that the films of today and tomorrow, whether written and produced in the East, in Europe or America had one thematic climax. It was apocalypse — doom — utter despair. Susan Sontag stressed that 16-and-17-year-olds were, if possible, even more pessimistic. J. Michael Allen, of Yale Divinity School, has said, "Students have fallen into terrible despair . . . so they're giving up. . . defeated, humiliated, and looking for a hiding place" in "drugs, communes, mysticism."

Here is why the return of Christ is such good news. In a crusade which I was conducting in Oregon, Professor Loyd Hayes asked me to speak and answer questions in three of his philosophy classes. In two of them, although I recollect having made no reference to the second advent of our Lord, bearded, beaded youths asked: "Do you believe that Jesus Christ is coming again?" There was obviously real excitement in these questions. It is our only philosophic hope.

Jesus forecast that there would be striking resemblances between men in Noah's time and those who lived just previous to His return. One which is relevant here, is that in the antediluvian era there were giants in the earth and the earth was filled with violence. They were intellectual giants to have advanced as rapidly as they did, yet violence overwhelmed them. Trevor Roper, the Oxford philosopher, reckons that man has undergone "a turning point," ushering in "a new age of violence in which" the whole world has capitulated to "a new character: a character of international anarchy." Scientists are telling us that the survival of civilization is being threatened by thermonuclear annihilation. Philosophers say anarchy will overturn us, if bombs do not get in ahead.

The philosophers of the past have tended to be theists. Today while scientists tend more and more to believe in God the philosophers who are most studied are, in intellectual posture, very often atheists. Immanuel Kant never attempted *a posteriori* to prove the existence of God, but believed in the necessity of believing in Him *a priori*. It was a subjective essential for man to believe in God. Regarding eternal life, Kant argued for immortality on the basis of heaven being necessary for the believer to develop fully his moral faculties. Schleiermacher,

Hegel, Ritschl, Dostoevsky, and Kierkegaard (the father of modern existentialism), were all devout believers in God. But today such of their successors as Jean Paul Sartre, the late Albert Camus, Julian Huxley, the late Bertrand Russell, Karl Jaspers and Martin Heidegger find it preferable to write from an atheistic stance. After all, their mentors Darwin, Freud and Marx were atheists, and their enormous influence upon twentieth-century life has been dominant in the whole area of modern thought, social structuring and conduct.

The escalating ascendancy of atheism is a philosophic sign that Jesus Christ will surely come again to assert, not only His existence and authority, but His salvation. For as surely as Nietzsche's "God is dead" theory, upon which Hitler intellectually built his thinking, ended up in the German philosopher going mad for the last fifteen years of his life, so the "God is dead" posturing of our times will leave man to the destructive ends of his own folly. Already in the Religion section of *Time*, an article on "The Death of the Death of God Theory" has appeared. In it the charter members of this movement admit that whereas on the surface side, the stone might read "God is dead," kicked up it declares that the whole of life is set in a religious context. Were Jesus Christ not to come again, there could be no salvation. St. Jude portended men "denying the only Lord God" (Jude 4). This would condition one-time Christian nations for the coming antichrist who shall "speak great words against the most High" (Daniel 7:25). Nor will he "regard the God of his fathers" (Daniel 11:37); who according to St. Paul "opposeth and exalteth himself above all that is called God" (2 Thessalonians 2:4).

Never before has a monolithic political system been superstructured on the foundation of atheism as has international Communism. Karl Marx insisted in his "Communist Manifesto" that his system could only operate on an atheistic base, and his thesis has been adhered to undeviatingly by Marxists throughout the world. Nobel prize-winning novelist Alexander Solzhenitsyn complains that he is unable to have the word "God" printed in capitalized form in the Soviet Union. The pattern Marxists have adopted is not immediately to uproot and exterminate the Church, but to wait until the time is propitious. It was only recently that Albania claimed to become "the first atheist state in the world," its *Nendori* reporting that 2,169 churches, monasteries, etc. had been closed and their adherents halted, even from minimal expressions of religion. China is near this stage. In Russia only 60,000 Bibles have been published since the takeover of Communism in 1917, nearly half of these being issued in 1926 and none during the last twelve years. One Russian told me that these had been circulated almost in their entirety outside Russia and were mere propaganda strokes. I had my three Bibles taken away from me at Moscow Airport when I entered Russia. Students in Red Square told me that churches were now looked upon as museums, and God was the fabricated opium of the capitalist overlords to keep their masses enslaved. One of Mao Tse-tung's sayings, which has been printed 700 million times over, is that "God is none other than the masses of the Chinese people. If they stand up and dig together with us, why can't these . . . mountains be moved away." As St. Paul forbode, "They have bartered away the true God for a false one, and have offered reverence and worship to created things instead of to the Creator, who is blessed forever; amen" (Romans 1:25, NEB).

What is perhaps much more alarming is the blatant atheism of the university people in the Western countries today. My Alma Mater, Oxford University, the last time I paid it a visit four or five years ago, had undergone a radical change over the previous five years. The Humanist Group, which militantly opposes religion in general and Christianity in particular, had grown during that time from a membership of fifty-two to over a thousand, which was more than all the religious societies combined. Their graduates infiltrate the key communications and political posts. The best-known British philosopher is Julian Huxley who arrogates, "God is no longer a useful hypothesis. A faint trace of God still broods over the world like the smile of a Cheshire cat, but psychological science will rub even that form from the universe." In Sweden, according to the recent Gallup poll, only 60 percent of the people now believe in a personal God.

North Americans are drifting in the same direction. In Canada two percent less of the people believe in God now than five years ago. There is a tremendous response to the Gospel on our university campuses today, but according to Bill Bright of Campus Crusade, 95 percent of American university and college students have no routine contact with any church. The kind of book which college students tend to read is the best seller, Russell Greenan's *It Happened in Boston,* presenting a bizarre character, who is a combination of a park bench dreamer, master painter and deranged narrator, who degenerates into a murderer and a plotter, anxious to kill God. Man is not sure that he could accomplish deicide, but he'd like to try. Atheistic legislation is moving much faster than its numbers warrant, as if it is being swept along by some diabolical force. The Louis Harris Poll claims that 78 percent of Americans believe that the U.S. Supreme Court was wrong in banning prayer from public schools. But the law stands despite this consensus to the contrary.

Many feel that the atheism which is rampant today is getting an assist, rather than a rebuttal, from the Church. Pope Paul laments the horizontalization of religion, which turns the Church into a social convenience rather than a spiritual force. God has been more and more depersonalized by theologians, who refer to Him merely as "the ground of being," "the force of life," "the principle of love," or "ultimate reality." This creates the impression of divesting Him of the capacity to be experienced and to establish and maintain a warm personalized relationship with His children through faith in Jesus Christ as Saviour and Lord. James McCord, President of Princeton Theological Seminary, laments that "Today, we are at the end of a theological era, with the old theological systems a shambles." Senator Frank Carlson said recently that "Not only have vast numbers of Americans lost all sense of the sacred, the moral, and the ethical, but the spiritual leaders from both the laity and the priesthood are often found in the forefront of this irreligious" retreat from sacred things. "The criticisms of God rank well above almost all other criticisms of the hour. More people — in more ways and on more occasions — cast doubt, hurl darts, and throw charges against God such as this country has never seen in all of its history."

And this atheism is getting through in the great American institutions. Not only has the Bible in particular, and Christianity in general, been barred from the school system but the United States Army has now ordered its chaplains to eliminate all reference to God and religious philosophy in lectures aimed at instilling moral responsibility in its soldiers — this as a result of the militant American Civil Liberties Union.

From Germany comes a Lutheran Church booklet, *Mit Einander für Einander Beten,* which deplores the fact that "the majority of our people are members of the Church, and are really unbelievers." A perusal of the widely-publicized Gallup Poll on religious beliefs of Europeans and North Americans reveals that an astonishing percentage of actual church members are atheists. That's like a child living at home who doesn't believe in mother.

Atheism as a philosophy of life is not content today to go its own way. Its proponents are getting more and more egotistical, haughty, militant and aggressively scornful of believers. This philosophic stance, the Scriptures teach, is indicative of the need for, and fact of, Christ's return. "Note this," anticipated St. Peter, that "in the last days there will come men who scoff at religion and live self-indulgent lives" (2 Peter 3:3, NEB). "You must remember, beloved, the predictions of the apostles of our Lord Jesus Christ," St. Jude forewarned, that "'In the last time there will be scoffers, following their own ungodly passions'" (Jude 17, 18, RSV). "In the last days," presaged St. Paul, men will be "heady, high-minded," "swollen with conceit." This is a time, unique in history, laments Pedro Arrupe, the head of the Jesuits, when the world is in the grip of a completely "godless society."

A glance at activities and student newspapers at universities and colleges reveals how the whole popular trend today is to hold the Church in derision. Essays, plays and novels use Christ's name constantly in profanity. The national news media carried accounts of how Jesus Christ was burned in effigy on the campus of a college whose pioneering president was America's greatest nineteenth-century revivalist. Student activists in California form a denomination of devil-worshipers, leaders of which are "Satan's

Ministers" who put on "devil's horns" and conduct services including nationally televised wedding ceremonies.

In Canada when Mrs. Madalyn Murray O'Hair, the American crusader for atheism as an official establishment, faced the nation recently in the television program, "Under Attack," thousands of students in one of the universities gave her repeated standing ovations; whereas when a clergyman was on, a few weeks later, they jeered. Why? Because "the carnal mind is at enmity against God" (Romans 8:7).

"The Graduate" is an example of a film which falls into this category. The hero at the end symbolically locks a wedding party in a church by barring the door with a gold crucifix, as if to say that there should be no further dialogue or interchange between an entirely secularized society and the Church. "Bedazzled" sets out categorically to challenge almost every basic Christian belief, exaggerating the purportedly outlandish things which are supposedly done by the Church to appease a capricious God. In "100 Rifles" the clergyman is seen as the foolish and mindless sycophant of whoever is in power. Reverence for God is at an all-time low. Jesus Christ and His Church are held up as the hangover symbols of an obsolete establishment. It seems to me that the whole movement toward nudity is a contemptuous scoffing at Jesus Christ who said, "If a man looks on a woman with a lustful eye, he has already committed adultery with her in his heart" (Matthew 5:28, NEB).

"Without God and without hope" philosophy must have a god. So into the vacuum steps Satan, "transformed into an angel of light." "Sympathy for the Devil" is a new film for 1971. When I was a rather sensitive undergraduate, to mention the "devil," or

"Satan" would be to incur derision and intellectually to invite a reputation for gross naïveté or unmitigated imbecility. Today the devil is openly doing a landslide business among youth and particularly on university campuses. "Satan Worshipers" are no joke. They are serious-minded, militantly on the march, and captivating a cross-section of the world's youth. Whole- and half-page newspaper write-ups, entire television programs, and leading magazine articles are devoted to propagating the movement. "The Process" (as their movement is sometimes known) is sharply on the increase. In one small city alone, early in 1971, 450 "ministers of Satan" were ordained. In Chicago at Easter, 1971, 4,000 gathered "to worship Satan." In England, the movement is so strong that a Member of Parliament claims 78 percent of secondary students have been in touch with a wizard or witch. According to the *Los Angeles Times,* whole villages in Russia are under the domination of wizards and witches. Voodoo is now as prevalent in Brazil as in the Congo. The movement, as reported by Toronto's Professor Tom Harpur is, in mid-1971, "worldwide." Its adherents who are amazingly with-it intellectually, believe "Satan . . . must be loved." It is ironic that the most definitive book yet written on the Satan movement is entitled: *The Second Coming: Satanism in America* by Arthur Lyons. The author, who is now a familiar figure on late-night talk-shows, makes the point: "The monster slouches toward Bethlehem to be born."

So is the mind free to think as it wills? That is, is it in neutral, or is it in reverse or drive? The Bible teaches that it is never in neutral. Either it is in the reverse gear of being under Satan's aegis, or it is shifted into drive by the liberation of Jesus Christ. At least the devil, philosophically, is out in the open these days. I remember when C. S. Lewis was around Oxford and Cambridge. He ate lunch most Mondays with my research supervisor. Lewis used to lament that the devil whom people denied intellectually was worse than the devil whom people of former times recognized. Today he is out in the open again.

One of Satan's instruments is "drugs." "When you follow your own wrong inclinations, your lives will produce evil results," wrote St. Paul to the Galatians, one of these being "spiritism" — also translated "witchcraft" and "sorcery." The word comes from the same Greek root as "pharmacy," possibly referring to the use of pharmaceutical drugs to induce psychic reactions. In Revelation 14, a whole people, we read, will fall under this "drugs" control. The diabolical spread of the drugs craze across the west is one of the tragic phenomena of our times. In May, 1971, the liberal BBC decided, in a Britain that has been lax on drug usage, to play no more pop songs which had mention — open or overt — of drugs. In the United States 1,000 a year die from heroin in New York City alone, to join the tragic ranks of the Jimi Hendrixes and the Janis Joplins. In the nation, deaths are up over 6,000 percent in a decade. Hauls of single allotments worth 35 million dollars are discovered. In Vietnam, 37,000 G.I.'s are found to be on heroin, according to the *New York Times,* and this the 95 percent pure variety (on the streets of America heroin is 5 percent pure on the average). President Nixon has decided to speed up the troop withdrawal in order that this pandemic might be put under control. He also plans to spend an estimated $155 million to finance a full-scale attack on the problem of narcotics abuse which, he states, "has assumed the dimensions of a national emergency." A White House aide reckons that there are 315,000 heroin addicts in the United States, and the numbers are growing like a plague. A *Playboy* poll of August, 1971, indicates that during the previous twelve months the percentage of American students who had smoked marijuana had risen from 47 percent to 62 percent.

Psychiatrists tell us that it will soon be possible to drug a whole nation and control its emotional responses. Already it is obvious to many what drug addiction can do, for example, to the old-fashioned American patriotism, which some of us used to detect as soon as we set foot in the United States. I used to wonder how modern man who had become so philosophically sophisticated could ever, eventually acquiesce to an antichrist. I wonder no more. We read: "This man of sin will come as Satan's tool, full of satanic power, and will trick everyone with strange demonstrations, and will pretend to do great miracles. He will completely fool those who are on their way to hell because they have said, 'No' to the truth; they have refused to believe it, and love it, and let it save them. So God will allow them to believe lies with all their hearts." President Nixon in mid-1971 goes so far as to point to "America's Public Enemy No. 1" as drug abuse.

Philosophically, is this vaunted atheism, this ribald scoffing, getting our generation anywhere? Dr. Irwin Moon reckons that more new facts are discovered by man today in 24 hours than in 2,000 years of ancient history. Yet, according to *Time,* which carries a cover story on contemporary philosophy, all is confusion, doubt and generally a vague and sickly gray.

"In the last days," prophesied St. Paul, people will be "always learning and yet never able to grasp the truth" (2 Timothy 3:7, Phillips). Why? Because they "defy the truth; they have lost the power to reason, and they cannot pass the tests of faith" (2

Timothy 3:8, NEB). No commentary could more accurately describe our generation of jaded intellectualism which is mired in the quicksands of sophisticated vagary. Of Sigmund Freud's original cloister of twelve satellite psychiatrists, seven committed suicide, saying to the world that the avant-garde ideas of the twentieth century simply did not bring fulfillment. The Schizophrenia Foundation of Psychiatrists in the United States now reveals that psychiatrists, who are supposed to have the answers for the problems of our generation, commit suicide at the rate of four times that of the general public. The times are "out of joint," as Shakespeare would say.

Whoever expected that guerrilla warfare involving murder and a threatened civil war would break out, of all places, on university campuses? San Francisco State to Kent State cost the American Government, for policing and troop interception, a hundred million dollars. *Time* features the campuses as places where "strikes and clashes with police supplanted studies." "The mindlessness" of it all, sighs the *Detroit Free Press*. Peter Thorneycroft, the English statesman, deplores the fact that even when students graduate today, many of them, for mercenary reasons, have no qualms about using their education to operate crime syndicates, while conforming to outward respectability in every other way, often robbing the government which provided them with the wherewithal to get an education.

The American sociologist, Dr. Ray Jeffrey, has demonstrated beyond all doubt that education escalates crime, if it is not accompanied by some moral or spiritual elevator. As of this writing the widely read philosopher, Jean Paul Sartre, is in a tangle with the French government over lawless attitude and actions. Albert Camus in his *Revolt* philosophically explained this intellectual malaise. It is no

longer a matter of the slave against his master, the
poor against the rich, but of man against creation.
It is a metaphysical revolt. Man is in a continual
state of tension. Nothing has either rhyme or reason.
Evil and virtue are mere chance and caprice. This is
illustrated in Philip Roth's best seller, *Portnoy's
Complaint,* in which Roth, who knew all about the
ethnic, sociological and Freudian hangups, yet is
still racked by guilt and tension: "torn by desires,
that are repugnant to my conscience and a conscience
repugnant to my desires."

The sequel to this is that man is not just pragmati-
cally, but philosophically, dishonest. "His word is
his bond," can no longer often be said. St. Paul predicted that in "the last days" men would be "trucebreakers" and "traitors." So morally irresponsible is
the human race becoming that Konrad Lorenz, the
writer on thermonuclear warfare, reckons that if
there is a missing link, it is more likely to be the
one between plants and animals, than between animals and humans, for man has, beneath his surface,
a beastly nature which could annihilate a whole section of humanity without batting an eyelash. At the
domestic level, we see unprecedented numbers of
"trucebreakers" and "traitors."

In Canada, the *United Church Observer* calculates
that what amounts to one in every twelve adults is
living "common law": that is, living with someone
who is not his legal life partner. Having gone to the
altar to be married, they simply ignore their vows
and become marital trucebreakers and traitors. *Pag-
eant* magazine reckons that in the United States,
"adultery seems to be as widely practiced as it must
have been in the orgiastic days before the flood."
And adultery is nearly always committed on the sly.
Ann Landers writes a pamphlet to try and assist
those who are victims of the matrimony, acrimony,

alimony treadmill, a very costly affair indeed. Marital infidelity is not new. But its blatant justification philosophically and even "theologically" is a phenomenon of our times. Professor Edward Hobbs, a theologian/philosopher of the University of California, conducts "Sexpo" seminars in which he recommends "extra-curricular sexual relations." I have never yet met a person who could feel secure and happy in a marriage in which this kind of trucebreaking and traitorism was practiced.

Duplicity is so widespread in the business world, that the *Canadian Magazine,* having polled employers, assesses that one in three workers is basically dishonest and cannot be trusted, if a thorough system of surveillance is not used. In F. H. Underhill's *In Search of Canadian Liberalism,* the author points out philosophically that the modern wave of liberalism which swept over the Western world is in "essence a Utopian faith" based on the innate goodness of "human nature." Modern psychologists have now, however, uncovered "deep subconscious instinctive drives in us which pervert our reason." We have been rudely awakened to the fact of our "original sin" which has issued in "outbursts of the demonic elements in human nature whose existence we had forgotten. We have learned to our horror the terrible potentialities of man's inhumanity to man." The two billion dollars worth of goods shoplifted and embezzled annually in the United States, most of it by people who are never prosecuted, demonstrates the duplicity of the average person.

Another philosophical sign that Jesus Christ is coming again is that our generation is replete with peace pretenders. Forecast St. Paul to the Thessalonians, "As far as times and seasons go, my brothers, you don't need written instructions. You are well aware that the day of the Lord will come as unexpectedly as a burglary to a householder. When men are saying, 'Peace and security,' catastrophe will sweep down upon them as suddenly and inescapably as birth pangs to a pregnant woman" (1 Thessalonians 5:1-3, Phillips). Jeremiah warned of those who say "peace, peace; when there is no peace" (Jeremiah 6:14). Let the record be kept straight. We are to strive for peace, and pray for peace. "If possible, so far as it lies with you, live at peace with all men" (Romans 12:18, NEB), exhorted St. Paul, and one of Jesus' beatitudes was "Blessed are the peacemakers." Indeed, St. Peter admonished believers that they "look forward to new heavens and a new earth, the home of justice. With this to look forward to, do your utmost to be found at peace" (2 Peter 3:13, 14, NEB). There is no want for peace pinings in our world today. Two thousand books have been written on the theme of peace since World War II. A Jewish rabbi writes on *Peace of Mind;* a Catholic bishop on *Peace of Soul* and Billy Graham on *Peace With God*. But with trucebreaking traitors and treasonists rife in our world (who will talk peace at the drop of a hat, then threaten to drop a thermonuclear bomb) we can be sure that nothing else will remedy this situation but the second coming of Jesus Christ.

Peace pretenders who wholesale peace propaganda populate our world today. For instance, on the very day in 1968 that the Russians were to have signed the pact for the banning of thermonuclear explosions, they invaded Czechoslovakia. They could say, "Peace, peace," out of one side of their mouths and declare war out of the other. And in the course of a single week in May, 1971, their leaders welcomed and signed a peace treaty with Trudeau, turned up in Prague to congratulate themselves for the 1968 invasion of Czechoslovakia; signed a solidarity pact with Egypt that they would support them to the hilt in another war with Israel, appealed to the United States for another nuclear ban (while sinking new 25-megaton bombs into their huge new silos); moved new weaponry into Ceylon in the Indian Ocean, and Cuba in the Caribbean; appealed to NATO for troop withdrawal from Europe, and sent two new nuclear submarines through the Dardanelles into the Mediterranean. That was quite a week for "peace, peace."

A few years ago, on the floor of the American Senate, a declaration made a quarter of a century earlier by the Secretary of the Executive Committee of the Comintern was read. Assured the Russian leader, "War to the hilt between Communism and Capitalism is inevitable. Today, of course, we are not strong enough to attack. Our time will come in twenty or thirty years. To win, we shall need the element of surprise. The bourgeoisie will have to be put to sleep. So we shall begin by launching the most spectacular peace move on record. There will be electrifying overtures and unheard of concessions. Capitalist countries, stupid and decadent, will rejoice to cooperate in their destruction. They will leap at another chance to be friends. As soon as their guard is down, we shall smash them with our clenched fists." With the current revival of Stalinism in Russia, the long-time dictator's resolve ought again to be quoted: "The object of Soviet Communism," asserted Stalin, "is 'victory of Communism throughout the world . . . by peace or war.' " I would like, as much as my secular contemporaries, to lapse into the current sentimental dream that all is well with the West and Communism today. But I am compelled by my reading of the Bible to say that this is simply not so. "Watch ye therefore!"

In Canada, according to the *Vancouver Province*, there are thirty-six front organizations for Marxism,

every one of which includes the word "peace."
Peace talks in Paris, discussing ways and means to
settle the Vietnam War have gone through nearly
100 fruitless sessions. Sometimes one watches televised goings-on in the United Nations and hears
more ignited notions than he sees united nations.
Perhaps the most bizarre peace propaganda ever, was
the bed-in campaign for peace by John Lennon, with
his acorns for peace being sent to the various world
heads of state with the accompanying note: "Please
plant these for peace" — as if world peace grows
on trees!

H. F. Armstrong, the longtime friend of Presidents,
published in mid-1971 his *Peace and Counterpeace:
from Wilson to Hitler* in which he describes how,
when he met Hitler in the '30's, Der Führer engaged
in a sixty-minute, nonstop monologue in which he
disclaimed any desire for war. He was a man of
peace. The world knows that he was soon the most
monstrous warmonger in history. His "peace, peace"
could have been translated "war, war." As the Psalm-
ist said: "When they say peace, war is in their heart."

Philosophically, much of the color running into
the smudged gray which is our moment of history,
must be put down to the cosmopolitanism of our
times. It is "a long twilight zone, year in and year
out," as John Kennedy put it in his Inauguration
Address. We are surrounded by milling millions who
want anonymity: "a world that is more and more
impersonal," as a lead editorial in the *Toronto Star*
noted. The Revelation of Jesus Christ (an "apocalyptic vision . . . more real" today than it has been
to "anyone since St. John on Patmos," as C. S.
Lewis puts it) foretold of how in the times of the
Lord's return, and those events leading up to it,
there would be 10,000 times 10,000 here, an army
of 200 million there, and a great number which

no man could number in another place. As Marshall McLuhan puts it, we shall soon be living in a "global village." A team of psychiatrists jointly write an article in a national weekly early in 1971 indicating that as population pressure builds up, there is no escape from a concurrent buildup of animal ferocity in human disguise. Man is like a volcano, about to erupt. Jamming the human race into a global ghetto will inevitably cause it to burst into a global conflagration. An American said to Mao Tse-tung recently that the Chinese are a "peace-loving people." "Oh!" replied Mao Tse-tung, "I think we are bellicose."

Martin Luther King, Jr., advanced the plea that "we must learn to live together as brothers, or we will die together as fools." Man seems utterly incapable of the former. Only the return of the King can supersede the latter.

Man has reacted to the enroachments and pressures of these cosmopolitan elements and gone on a hedonistic pleasure binge, and the trend is bound to accelerate. Walter Reuther told Billy Graham that in twenty years, it will be possible in a single year to produce one hundred times as much steel by one-hundredth the manpower. People will only need to work, at most, two days a week — perhaps less. The result of all this is surfeited pleasure hunting, leading to "misery" and "wretchedness," signs of Christ's promised coming again. St. James spoke of the "last days" being a time when "rich men weep and howl for your miseries" (James 5:1), and what makes it doubly sad is that St. John envisaged that men would be insensitive to the fact that they were "wretched" and "miserable" despite the fact that they were "rich and increased in goods."

John Barth, the American novelist, expresses the philosophic dilemma of our times in the title of his newest novel, *Lost in the Funhouse*. People are trying to crowd into a syndrome of joytoys, a sort of funhouse to escape the stark realities of life, only to find themselves lost. Wrote the philosopher, Bertrand Russell, "I could think of nothing but suicide," and of the world around him, "over man and all his works, night falls pitiless and dark." As James Russell Lowell despaired, "life's emblem deep: a confused noise between two silences," so people in top echelons everywhere are feeling. Eric Burden, lead singer of the world-famous rock group, the Animals, is quoted as sighing, "I feel old and frustrated." As the top pop of the last five years goes, "I Can't Get No Satisfaction"; and one of the Rolling Stones who popularized it demonstrates his song by killing himself in his own backyard. It reflects the philosophic despair of so many millions of teen-agers. In my writings elsewhere, I quote from scores of current pop songs, which express the absolute despair and inconsolable loneliness of our generation of youth. And it can do nothing but get worse. Says Fulton Sheen in early 1971: "Our delinquent youths in America become delinquent because they have no missions, no purpose in life. Pour steam into a boiler and give it no work, and it will blow up. Youth is blowing up for the same reason." Think of what will happen when they only work a day or two each week!

Helen Hutchinson in her book review column reveals that the best-selling books currently are those dealing with Psycho-Cybernetics because of the "gnawing dissatisfaction with life that obviously plagues too many people." A friend of mine twenty years ago has emerged as what the *Toronto Star* calls "the conglomerate king of Canada," meaning that he is now our country's most flourishing businessman. Some months ago he was in a meeting in which I preached in one of our great cities. We chatted afterwards. He expressed how much the Gospel of Jesus Christ is needed by lonely businessmen. He suggested we meet over a meal sometime and discuss this whole matter of fulfillment in Christ. Life without God is too much in these modern times of stress and strain.

*The Sunday Telegraph* in London was responsible along with the Gallup International Poll for the recent probing of the decline in Christian faith in Europe and the United States. The results were widely publicized and, as already stated, depressing. Under "Main Conclusions," the *Telegraph* assessed, "Religious beliefs are declining, morals also have slumped, honesty is on the wane, happiness is becoming increasingly hard to find, peace of mind is rare." The British Brains' Trust, appearing on BBC-TV, agreed unanimously that tragedy outlasts comedy because life is tragedy. And the *New York Times* claims that in 1971 humor has all but gone out of the American way of life.

Since God is love, it would not be right if Jesus Christ did not come back again and bring us into a state of philosophic fulfillment. The suicide rates of both the United States and the United Kingdom yield the facts that about eight times as many rich as poor, per capita; eight times as many highly educated as normally-schooled, per capita; and eight times as many of those at the center of the "good-time" life as those at the drab fringes commit suicide. Philosophically reduced to a formula, this reads that the more people earn, the more they learn and the more they burn, the more they yearn for fulfillment. This throws the whole of our value scales back into the melting pot for reevaluation, especially when according to Ann Landers' column, suicide probably would be in fourth place as a cause of death, if all the facts were known.

The sophisticated Broadway musical, "Hair,"

features a nude scene and a female singing that
we've got eyes, ears, teeth and hair, but what we've
really got is trouble and sorrow. This is life! Is it
any wonder that actors and actresses take an astrol-
oger around with them to consult "their lucky stars"?
The thematic question is, as with so many modern
plots: "Where do I go?" The obvious conclusion,
from a Christian point of view, is that men need
Jesus Christ to come into their hearts, and they need
Him to come to earth again and "re-environmentalize"
us with Himself.

While this emptiness within is a characteristic of
our times, the pressure from without is another sign
that Jesus Christ is coming. Our Lord forecast that
prior to His return there would be "distress of nations, with perplexity," that is, whole "nations will
stand helpless, not knowing which way to turn,"
intimidated with "terror at the thought of all that is
coming upon the world; for the celestial powers
will be shaken. And then they will see the Son of
Man coming on a cloud with great power and glory.
When all this begins to happen, stand upright and
hold your heads high, because your liberation is
near" (Luke 21:25-28, NEB). These last two sen-
tences make the philosophic posture of believers a
most auspicious thing. But a world which is depend-
ing on any other hope than that afforded by Jesus
Christ cannot be realistic and optimistic at the same
time.

Mrs. Golda Meir, Israeli Premier, says that she
occupies her office with a "constant feeling of terror."
In Canada, the Prime Minister meets the premiers
from the ten provinces, and the most-read news
magazine features our national problems as so com-
plex "that the object seemed to be to disagree almost
to the point of destructiveness." Canada, as the
world knows from the events of 1970, is closer to

disintegration than at any time in its 100-year history. When an American Secretary of Defense committed suicide because of unendurable pressures, he reasoned, "This state of tension will continue for the rest of our lives, and those of our children."

"We have to ask ourselves," writes Walter Lippmann, "why do we find ourselves facing impossible choices wherever we turn?" Newspaper columns read: "Fatal Objections Were Found to Almost Every Decisive Step!"; "Cultivated Uncertainty Is the Order of the Day"; "Inexpressible Consternation!"; "Both Were Alike in Not Knowing Which Way to Turn or What to Do!"; "No Normalcy!" Philosopher C. E. M. Joad, formerly of Cambridge and famous for his appearances on the British Brains' Trust, reasoned, "You don't give your children dangerous toys until you know that they can handle them. But this is in fact what science has done." It has given man the wherewithal to exterminate himself at a time of tragically declining moral responsibility. Is it therefore surprising then, that in the United States the National Committee for an Effective Congress cautions that at "all levels of American life," it is increasingly evident "that the country may, in fact, be suffering from a kind of national nervous breakdown?"

This "distress with perplexity" is present in the academic world. Murray Ross, President of York University in Toronto, resigns, saying that no university president can today hope to endure the pressures for more than ten years. And Claude Bissell, President of the University of Toronto (Canada's largest) follows suit. Three hundred college presidencies and one thousand deanships stand vacant in the United States. President Johnson, contrary to all speculation, resigned in 1968. Pope Paul VI talks of being the first modern pope to resign. Rumors that

Queen Elizabeth of England will resign keep circulating. Today's pressures are getting to be too much for people.

Jesus said that this accumulative distress and perplexity would have a physical effect on the human race: "men's hearts failing them for fear" (Luke 21:26). There have always been isolated instances of people in society living in fear: like the Kansan who is currently so afraid of the roads that he loads his Rolls Royce onto a flat car and rides on the rails. But the shocking increase in deaths from heart failure in our generation, throughout the world, is not an isolated phenomenon: a Scottish physician says there has been a 900 percent increase of heart failure in this generation in Scotland; an Atlanta heart specialist is quoted as placing it at 400 percent in the United States. Murray Robertson of the Ontario Heart Foundation says that heart disease, the number one killer of Canadians, is an "epidemic of the 20th century." Nor does any physician look upon the heart transplant as the ultimate solution. Of 100 or more heart transplants performed throughout the world, only two have survived for a year or more. Pressures are increasing. A national TV program is entitled "Man Afraid." "The fact is that today the biggest single emotion which dominates our lives is fear," comments *U.S. News and World Report*. "I write this to frighten you," writes the Nobel Prize winner, Professor Urey, assuring us, "I am a frightened man myself. All the scientists I know are frightened — frightened for their lives — and frightened for your life."

Much more than annihilation fears build pressures that lead to heart failure. The *New York Times* explains, "Throughout the entire world," the "issues that formerly took a century or more to come to a boil are in constant eruption. Everything is being bunched up — time, space, nations, peoples, issues. And everything has a fuse attached to it. The habits of nations, always variable, have become starkly irrational." Comments Kevin White, the Mayor of Boston in 1971: "I think the most frustrating thing for new mayors is not being able to solve the problems of their cities. Many of them are quitting after one term these days."

I have been around the world three times with visits to 100 countries in the last five years. We sometimes tend to think of Vietnam as being the only war in the world today. But one sees trouble spots everywhere he goes. There are five wars going on in the Middle East alone, in 1971, not to mention innumerable wars in Africa and even South America. An Indian said to me in June, 1971, that he grows weary of hearing of nothing but Vietnam, when, in East Pakistan and India, there are at least 25 being slaughtered to every one who is killed in Vietnam. Each country has its national crisis, it seems, driving its leaders to distraction. Dr. Sherwood Wirt, editor of *Decision,* returns from Southeast Asia and describes how Indonesia and Singapore are at loggerheads, as are the Philippines and Malaysia; Thailand and Cambodia; Pakistan and India, *ad infinitum nauseum.* Who, five years ago, would have believed that in 1970 Prime Minister Trudeau of Canada would have had to utilize the War Measures Act? Dr. Roy Grinker of the Michael Reese Hospital in Chicago comments on how these strains affect the heart, and how the terrific pressures of the age we live in overload our coronary organs far beyond nature's provision. It was most necessary then that Jesus made His statements, "Let not your heart be troubled" (John 14:1), and "Settle it therefore in your hearts," in connection with His return, so that His disciples might have fortification.

"Trauma: the leading cause of death among Americans between ages 1 and 37" headlines a national magazine in 1970. This should not be so of Christians.

Paul Johnson of the sophisticated *New Statesman* in London, after reviewing the despairing facts of a world gone out of control concluded, "There are times when I feel that I would welcome an invasion from Mars." That, Mr. Johnson, is the way the whole world feels philosophically. But the invasion will not take place from Mars. It will be the return of Jesus Christ, the "desire of all people," whether or not people know it, as the ancient prophet prognosticated. How can we solve our deep philosophic apprehensions? Robert Browning averred, "shooting at fear with all the strength of hope." "We are saved by hope," affirmed St. Paul.

Why does the whole world not read the signs of the times and believe? *Intelligence Digest* of London reviewing the plight of the times reasons: "If not in present conditions, in what circumstances can people be roused?" As St. Peter projected, a sign of the coming of the Lord is that men would be "willingly ignorant." Jesus in relating Dives' appeal from hell declared that if men are impenitent, even one's rising from the dead to testify of the unseen world would not induce repentance. Affirmed the great philosopher, Immanuel Kant, "There is nothing good in the world or the universe which does not begin with the good will." The will is the hinge upon which the kingdom of God swings open. "If there be first a willing mind," St. Paul assured the Corinthians, "it is accepted according to that a man hath, and not according to that he hath not" (2 Corinthians 8:12). Henry Ward Beecher said there are only two classes of people in the world: the whosoever wills and the whosoever won'ts.

Man need not be ignorant of the way to heaven. In that passage on the return of Christ in 1 Thessalonians 4, which Cardinal Cushing read at the funeral of President Kennedy, St. Paul urges, "I would not have you ignorant." He then defines the basis of salvation and how we can go when Christ comes again: "Believe that Jesus died and rose again" for in this "we have a definite message from the Lord." To those who accept Jesus Christ on this basis as their Saviour and Lord is the assurance given, that they can surely know they will be His at His coming, and forthwith forever.

# Chapter Five

# The Church and the Coming Christ

The New Testament leaves us little doubt as to what would be the distinguishing characteristics of the organized or visible Church at the time of Christ's second advent. Our Lord's first concern in this world is His Church. After all, "He loved it and gave Himself for it." Those of us who are its ministers should have that same love for the Church. Like Hermes, we exclaim, "The Church, this miracle of Earth."

In history, no institution can be compared with the record of the Church for teaching and character building. The very ribs of our democratic society are the Ten Commandments. In every country where Christianity has been abandoned, barbarism has resulted. Substituting material law for Christian law has put a million peasants to death by cruel and calculated starvation and non-Aryans by the millions, in the Nazi gas chamber. This was done by highly sophisticated people who had rejected the Church. On the other hand, the Church has endured through 20 centuries, building up an immense body of goodwill born of 10,000 philanthropies; a network of missionary outposts unsurpassed by any organization in the world; an incomparable heritage of literature, art, and music; a long record of opposing tyranny; an ever-improving teaching apparatus and most important of all, the person and teachings of Jesus Christ.

But truth is truth and the Church is currently in a state of decline. No one grieved more than our Lord that the Church would fall into appalling decay prior to His coming. Indeed this is the primary reason for His coming. The Beatles are not alone in wagering that the Church if it continues in its present plight will go out of operation before this century ends. Our Lord must come again to rectify this state of affairs. When He will come, we do not know. But that He will, no true Christian can doubt.

In the first place, St. Paul made it unmistakably clear that "in the last days" men will "preserve the outward form of religion, but are a standing denial of its reality" (2 Timothy 3:5, NEB). The paradox which the agnostic Pierre Berton describes in his best-selling *The Comfortable Pew*, is that while the polls reveal that almost everyone — some 94 per cent — believes in God, accepts the doctrine of the virgin birth, and life after death, and is convinced of the power of prayer, so few churchgoers seem really to be Christian. Sometimes we have to ask a non-believer what he expects of a Christian to get a clearer view of what a Christian should be. Albert Camus averred that "What the world expects is that the Christian should speak out loud and clear and pay up personally." That's a tall order coming from an atheistic existentialist, whose writings run in anything but a Christian stream. Or H. G. Wells, the historian, who ended up observing that "The world is now a very tragic and anxious world ... more people are asking today (than ever before) and asking with a new intensity, 'What must I do to be saved?' The trouble with the Christian churches is that they give a confused, unconvincing and unsatisfying answer."

A former editor of *McLean's* magazine tells of a series of Holy Week services, held in an Ontario city. Five clergymen, old friends, sat until the early hours of the morning discussing the problems of the ministry, sipping coffee, and generally talking shop. Suddenly one of the men interjected the remark, "I'll have to confess that if someone came and asked me point-blank how he could find God, I simply wouldn't know what to say." Then looking around at the others, he said, "And am I wrong in saying that the same would be true of the rest of you?" There was an extended silence but no rebuttal.

From within, Dr. Verghese, as Assistant Secretary General of the World Council of Churches, reckons that this "form of godliness without the power thereof" exists because we in the Church have too often tried to get people to act like Christians who have never committed their lives to Christ. Instead of reality, we have form. It is noteworthy that *Time* quotes a United Presbyterian minister in 1971 who objects vigorously to the Jesus People movement on the basis: "I thought we'd outgrown that. I'd like to see some kind of form." According to St. Paul, the lapse into a "form of godliness without the power thereof" is to be a sign of the church as the end nears.

One of Hollywood's most sensual stars, supported by a chorus of swinging, sparsely-draped girls, belts out, "I'm saved, Oh, yes, I'm saved! My soul is saved!" One cannot help but ask, "Saved from what?" "The Graduate" is one of the avant-garde films. It features, "And here's to you, Mrs. Robinson, Jesus loves you more than you will know — Ho, Ho, Ho! Heaven holds a place for those who pray! Hey, Hey, Hey!" Surely this is "a façade of 'religion,' but their conduct will deny its validity." According to Leslie Steffard, the British author, the word "Christian" has become one of the vaguest words in the English language. "The church of today," says a leading psychologist, "is like an autumn leaf, dry and dead but retaining its form and structure."

Prior to His coming and the end of the age, Jesus cautioned His disciples that ". . . the love of many shall wax cold" (Matthew 24:12). St. Paul described how in the last days, folk would be ". . . loving all the time what gives them pleasure instead of loving God" (2 Timothy 3:4, Phillips). Worshipers in whom love for God is replaced by love for pleasures, are inevitably a people like those in the church in Laodicea, to whom our Lord said, "You are neither cold nor hot. I could wish that you were either cold or hot!" A chosen generation is too often a frozen generation today, too frequently as straight as a gun barrel, but just as empty; a bit at times like the moon, which radiates a light but gives off no heat, and even that light is occasionally darkness when the world comes between it and the sun.

Jude was writing at the conclusion of his letter to believers "in the last time." "But you, my friends, must fortify yourselves in your most sacred faith. Continue to pray in the power of the Holy Spirit. Keep yourselves in the love of God, and look forward to the day when our Lord Jesus Christ . . . will give eternal life" (Jude 20, 21, NEB). St. Peter in his treatment of conditions as they would exist at the day of the Lord, spoke of "slackness." This loss of love, this reluctance to be either hot or cold, this slackness on the part of the Church is all around us.

*Look* describes contemporary "Christianity in retreat": how, over the last decade there has been a steady decline in membership and attendance, in inverse ratio to the population increase. The Church has become "largely complacent and irrelevant" and "instead of being a goad is largely at peace with society." Billy Sunday once remarked aptly that there wouldn't be so many non-going church members, if there weren't so many non-going churches. The world expects the church to have a message, a message it too often simply does not have.

When the World Council of Churches was founded in 1948, one of its conscientious supporters enthused, "by power of gathered numbers, the mightily organized church will move irresistibly to overcome the world by application of Gospel principles." Visser't Hooft, for nearly all of its existence the Secretary-General of the World Council of Churches, characterizes the Church today: "confusion reigns supreme — politically, theologically, socially."

To the British novelist, John Braine, the powerlessness of the Church lies in the fact that it "needs to make up its mind. Its trouble stems from the fact that nobody seems to know exactly what it stands for." When the Gospel is preached with authority, relevance, simplicity and in its intrinsic purity, it will attract people, revolutionize them and send them forth to live meaningful and directed lives. However, when it is diluted, vague, impersonal and smug, it is not fulfilling its mission. Here, too, is why the second advent is so little mentioned in its teaching. The reason for this neglect according to C. S. Lewis is that church members are so comfortable in this world that they cannot bring themselves to think about going to another.

The consequence of this loss of love and slackness is what the Scriptures call a "falling away." "Let no man deceive you by any means:" wrote St. Paul to the Thessalonians, "for that day shall not come, except there come a falling away first. . ." (2 Thessalonians 2:3). St. Peter concludes the third chapter of his second Epistle in which he outlines the apocalyptic judgments of "the day of the Lord" with the

appeal, "But you, my friends whom I love, are forewarned, and should therefore be very careful not to
. . . lose your proper foothold" (2 Peter 3:17, Phillips). *Look* describes the Church of England: "con-
firmations have dropped by a quarter in the last few
years, candidates for ordination, by over a third in
the last year. The 14,500 Anglican churches are
more often relics of the past, than signposts to the
future. Church attendance in the United States in
one year has dropped 2 percent, and over the last
dozen years a full 10 percent. In Toronto, while
the population of Metro has increased 16 percent
over a five-year period, membership in the one
hundred fifty-two churches of the Toronto Presbytery
of the United Church of Canada has dropped 5 percent and what is much more a reason for pessimism,
Sunday School enrollment has declined by one-third.

Not only is there a falling away from the Church
in Britain, America and Canada, but throughout the
world. Active Protestants, for example, in 1830
numbered 200 million of 800 million people who
lived in the world. Today, with 4½ times the population, active Protestants still only number 200 million. There are a million towns in the free world
without any evangelical churches. There are 36,000
vacancies waiting to be filled on foreign mission
fields. *Christianity Today* informs us that there are
only 28,486 active American Protestant missionaries,
so that it can be seen that the ranks of workers are
appallingly depleted. Some say: but the American
Peace Corps and similar organizations are taking the
place of missionaries. They may be socially, but
spiritually, the Peace Corps has to be dead, because
its first principle is that its recruits will not try to
change the religion of the peoples with whom they
work. Without spiritual motivation, is it any wonder
that, in mid-1971, the Peace Corps is asked to leave

Peru, because some of its personnel are drug addicts? Did you ever hear of American missionaries being ejected from a country on drug charges?

The result of all this is that there are thirty times as many babies being born annually into the world as there are people joining all the Christian churches combined, including, of course, Catholic and Orthodox. It is estimated that if the present trend continues, by the end of the century only 2 percent of the human race will be Christian. I suggest that if we believe the Christian Gospel to be valid, Jesus Christ would be less than God the Son, if He did not return to correct this situation.

Much of the blame for this falling away from the Church, must be put down to the unholiness of the Church itself, a condition which Jesus and His apostles clearly predicted would exist. Prior to His coming and the end of the age, Jesus said that "iniquity shall abound." ". . . imposters" in the church, wrote St. Paul to Timothy "will go on from bad to worse, deceivers and deceived" (2 Timothy 3:13, RSV). It is a painful thing to have to point out the fulfillments around us of these predictions. According to *Time,* one ecclesiastical body publishes a magazine which contains so much obscenity that it drives Roy and Dale Rogers right out of their church. We pick up our papers and see where a prominent Episcopal bishop is unfrocked for chronic immorality, indecent sex suggestions and habitual drunkenness.

Every major denomination has its ranks depleted, with increasing frequency, by this sort of thing. From Wisconsin comes the news that, in a church, a play "Paradise Now" was staged in which nearly nude performers inspired the audience to strip. Two females and five males did so completely. What do we expect society at large to do, when this kind of thing goes on in a church? In Ontario, a minister is exposed, not merely for permitting, but for reportedly promoting, pre-marital sex relations on the church premises. "In the final age," forewarned St. Jude, "there will be men who pour scorn on religion, and follow their own godless lusts." These men "split communities, for they are led by human emotions and never by the Spirit of God." English Rector Stephan Hopkinson reckons that the Christian Church ought to put its approval upon homosexuality and suicide. A Unitarian clergyman in Alberta gets national publicity by promoting in his "church" physical communion services, in which members are invited to come in bikinis and push together like shocks of sheaves, until they feel the full emotional impact of physical fellowship. Anyone with normal human responses knows the outcome of that kind of "communion." A Council of Churches commissions and pays for a film in which clergymen take off their clothes and face the congregation in the buff and the naked body of an attractive young woman is passed around from man to man as a form of "communion." Church members are being urged to move toward Sodom. St. Peter described how "there shall be" those who ". . . turn back and abandon the sacred commandments delivered to them! For them the proverb has proved true: 'The dog returns to its own vomit,' and, 'The sow after a wash rolls in the mud again' " (2 Peter 2:21, 22, NEB).

Moral lapses and accidents have always occurred in the history of the church, but this sort of thing being sponsored by churchmen is something previous generations simply could not have credited. "After 2,000 years of Christianity," bemoans the British peer, Lord Halifax, the peoples of Christendom have "lapsed into degradation of the worst kind of paganism, as if men have no further use for Christianity."

What is conceivably worse than unholiness in the Church is hypocrisy. "God's Spirit specifically tells us that in later days," wrote St. Paul in his first letter to Timothy, "there will be . . . teachings given by men who are lying hypocrites" (1 Timothy 4:1, 2, Phillips). Nothing is so ludicrous as to try and build a church from stumblingblocks. Too many in the Church are like straight pins: they point one way but head the other. One of the most eloquent, if tragic, passages in the entire New Testament is where Jude is forecasting of those "in the last time" who would be ". . . a menace to the good fellowship of your feasts, for they eat in your company without a qualm yet they care for no one but themselves. They are like clouds driven up by the wind, but they bring no rain. They are like trees with the leaves of autumn but without a single fruit — they are doubly dead, for they have no roots either. They are like raging waves of the sea producing only the spume of their own shameful deeds. They are like stars which follow no orbit, and their proper place is the everlasting blackness of the regions beyond the light" (Jude 12, 13, Phillips).

Religion is the best armor a man can have, but it is the worst cloak. It is a most disastrous route which leads by the communion table to perdition.

Jesus in that set of seven parables, as recorded in Matthew 13, gave two which left no mistake as to the exposure of hypocrites, when He comes again. The one was of the wheat and the tares, and the other states that "The kingdom of Heaven is like a net let down into the sea, where fish of every kind were caught in it. When it was full, it was dragged ashore. Then the men sat down and collected the good fish into pails and threw the worthless away. That is how it will be at the end of time. The angels will go forth, and they will separate the wicked from the good, and throw them into the blazing furnace, the place of wailing and grinding of teeth" (Matthew 13:47-50, NEB).

George Bernard Shaw was no friend of the Church. One of his really telling indictments against hypocrites was that the trouble with Jesus Christ was that He had disciples. Why is the Church failing more and more to live up to its profession? According to Biblical forecast, it is because of its departure from the historic faith. It is not because of its irrelevance, but because of its irreverence. "Now the Spirit speaketh expressly," wrote St. Paul to Timothy "that in the latter times some shall depart from the faith, giving heed to seducing spirits. . ." (1 Timothy 4:1). ". . . incapable of reaching a knowledge of the truth," Paul writes later, ". . . these men defy the truth; they have lost the power to reason, and they cannot pass the tests of faith" (2 Timothy 3:7, 8, NEB).

"A phenomenon of today's young candidates for the ministry," observes *Life,* "is that a great many of them do not have a positive acceptance that Jesus Christ is the Son of God." The late Bishop James Pike described in an internationally read magazine how he "jettisoned the trinity, the virgin birth and the resurrection" of Jesus Christ. We could commiserate with him in his distress, but is this not precisely why he was "giving heed to seducing spirits," by involving himself on a national television network in a spiritistic seance? The secularization of the Church, as Pope Paul has been pointing out again and again, is one of the travesties of our time.

Dr. Howard Clark, Anglican Primate of Canada addresses the Lambeth Conference of Bishops in London on one of the regrettable results of overzealous ecumenism. It is the compromises we are making toward a rationalism which is secularizing our faith: "Is it any wonder," asks the Primate, "that we have lost the power to communicate to the secular, unbelieving world the deep truths about God that are in our Christian tradition?"

Two major Canadian denominations contemplate a merger. Early in 1971 they have concurrent, contiguous national gatherings at the honeymoon capital of North America, Niagara Falls. They presage their merger with the publication of a new hymnal — one which attempts to edit out "obsolete" hymns, and replace them with ones which will communicate to young people. Remarks by one clergyman to another were overheard by a newsman: "Strange isn't it, that we put in songs on the euphoria of the modern dance and the sacrament of sex, while removing such old timers as 'Amazing Grace.' With 'Amazing Grace' at the top of the charts this week, it seems to me that what we don't think will communicate to our youth, communicates to them very well!"

". . . I feel compelled," wrote St. Jude to saints (some of whom would live "in the last times,") "to make my letter to you an earnest appeal to put up a real fight for the faith which has been once for all committed to those who belong to Christ" (Jude 3, Phillips). This does not mean that we are to fight each other, or discriminate against those who belong to other branches of the Christian Church. It means "fight the good fight of faith," as St. Paul exhorted his protegé, Timothy.

Not content merely to deny the faith, the apostles predicted that many, as the end approached, would be deliberately and even aggressively apostate, contriving to incite others to be hostile to the historic Christian faith. "First of all you must realize that in the last days mockers will undoubtedly come," wrote St. Peter in the last of his recorded chapters, ". . . and they will say, 'What has happened to his promised coming? Since the first Christians fell asleep, everything remains exactly as it was since the beginning of creation!' They are deliberately shutting their eyes to a fact that they know very well" (2 Peter 3:3-5, Phillips). St. Paul, in the last of his recorded chapters carried the same concern: "I adjure you by his coming," that "the time will come when they will not stand wholesome teaching, but will follow their own fancy and gather a crowd of teachers to tickle their ears. They will stop their ears to the truth and turn to mythology" (2 Timothy 4:1, 3, NEB).

Possibly Jeane Dixon (in *A Gift of Prophecy*) is right in predicting the infiltration of treason into the clergy of all denominations. One of the most remarkable pieces of literature which I have recently read was the address given by the former editor of *Punch* (London), Malcolm Muggeridge, in The High Kirk of St. Giles to the students of the University of Edinburgh, of which he served as Rector. Having undergone a striking Christian conversion, his address was a "straightforward confession of faith" in Jesus Christ as Lord, entitled, "Another King." In it he makes this astonishing statement: "As far as I am concerned, it is Christ or nothing," adding, "What I have just said is, I know, far more repellent to most of the present ecclesiastical establishment than any profession of skepticism or disbelief."

Just how little some churchmen are concerned to preserve or fend for the deity of Christ is evidenced in the fact that one American Episcopal bishop would like to scrap the Lambeth Conferences, the World Council of Churches and the Roman Catholic Church in favor of a world religious organization which would put Buddha, Mohammed and possibly Mao Tse-tung on a par with Christ. Men have said things like this before, but they have not done so and retained office in an orthodox Christian denomination. I am personally acquainted with a famous English bishop who, despite Jesus' insistence on, "You must be born again," requests "Count me among the once born men." It seems to me that Archbishop Michael Ramsay was not exaggerating when he suggested, "Let African and Asian missionaries come to England to help to convert the post-Christian heathenism in our country."

The apostles forecast that militant apostasy would eventually reach blasphemous proportions. "In the last days," wrote St. Paul, there will be "blasphemers." St. Peter predicted that the very worst possible theological position the church could take would be adopted by some: ". . . there shall be false teachers among you, who privily shall bring in damnable heresies, even denying the Lord that bought them" (2 Peter 2:1). This to St. Peter (St. Jude wrote almost exactly the same thing), was the absolute nadir. No one could go further down.

"People today," writes a churchman in a widely circulated magazine, "have no interest in the emotionalism of the cross and Christ's shed blood." One asks if men like these have experienced the efficacy of the cross. Obviously not. The tragedy, St. Peter further forecasts, would be that "they will gain many adherents to their dissolute practices, through whom the true way will be brought into disrepute" (2 Peter 2:2, NEB). As for the consequence to themselves? Their "judgment now of a long time lingereth not, and their damnation slumbereth not" (2 Peter 2:3).

"Jesus was the son of a Roman soldier," writes one American bishop, and "to worship Christ" is "rank idolatry." Even a non-churchman like Abraham Lincoln affirmed, "I know that liberty is right, for Christ teaches it, and Christ is God."

If people in (or outside) the Church will not worship Jesus Christ as their Messiah, then they must construct some other messiah. An American churchman writes in a national magazine that "Gunsmoke's" marshal, Matt Dillon (Jim Arness), Ben Cartwright of "Bonanza" (Lorne Green), and "Ironside" (Raymond Burr) represent "Messiah-like" figures. "Each of these characters represents a fragment, however tiny, of Christ." Our Lord cautioned us about this, forecasting that prior to His coming "If anyone says to you then, 'Look here is Christ!' or 'There he is!' don't believe it. False Christs and false prophets are going to appear . . ." (Matthew 24:23, 24, Phillips).

The aging apostle John was very emphatic about this: ". . . every spirit that acknowledges the fact that Jesus Christ actually became man, comes from God, but the spirit which denies this fact does not come from God. The latter comes from the antichrist . . ." (1 John 4:2, 3, Phillips). When I was a lad, it was unheard of, but today, the world over, media people refer to certain meteoric and magnetic personalities as "messiahs" with super "charisma." And one scarcely ever reads through a magazine or newspaper without some reference somewhere to a Joe Namath, a Muhammad Ali, a Bobby Orr, a De Gaulle, a Pierre Trudeau, a John Lindsay, a John Lennon, a James Taylor, or a Timothy Leary being referred to as a "messiah" with "charisma." Never have so many Americans been served up such protracted press coverage of a murder trial as was given to the Sharon Tate case, all because some "messiah-starved" females thought Charles Manson was their "Christ." The Long Island University professor, who went to China on the ping-pong trip, had one dominant impression of that fascinating society. It was a people galvanized by the totally dominant Mao Tse-tung messiahship, the Jesus Christ of Red China.

Tolstoy the Russian stated that every man has in

him a God-shaped blank. Another Russian, Dostoevski, put it even more vividly: "So long as man remains, he strives for nothing so incessantly and so painfully as to find someone to worship." If a nominal Christian rejects orthodox Christianity, he will not live in a religious vacuum. He will create a new religion, complete with messiah and the ritualistic trappings to go along with it. Erich Fromm, writing on the reason for the outbreaks of violence, explains it in terms of Americans having in so many instances abandoned their Christian beliefs, and consequently they are caught in the transition of searching for a replacement. Some "messiah" appears and they'll chase him even though he is a real charlatan.

Jesus saw people during His incarnation as He sees them today, fainting, scattered abroad, and as sheep without a shepherd. "Nothing reflects confusion more than a flock of sheep without a shepherd," writes L. Nelson Bell, Executive Editor of *Christianity Today*. "Beset by barking dogs, frustrated by one another and by the natural obstacles around them, leaderless sheep will mill about in a frenzy of indecision, unable to cope with the problems that confront them." This is why every sheep demands a shepherd. It is why every man must have a messiah: real or imagined. A brilliant writer told me recently that he is convinced that everything a man does reflects his religious nature, for essentially he is chronically and eternally religious. He cited the latest university craze: to establish departments of parapsychology in every sophisticated institution of higher learning, including those in Russia.

Finally, concerning the Church and the coming of Christ, two points need highlighting. The period preceding the second advent of Christ would for the Church be a time of unprecedented persecution, and of great evangelistic harvest, for I do not believe that our Lord will come for an utterly defeated Church. It will be a time of grave persecution. In the last days, wrote St. Paul to Timothy, "Persecution is inevitable for those who are determined to live really Christian lives, while wicked and deceitful men will go from bad to worse..." (2 Timothy 3:12, 13, Phillips).

*Time* recently described how the Reds "are keeping in jail tens of thousands of Christians in Red China, Russia and other countries. They torture them. They take children away from their parents if they teach them Christianity." *Look* says that in Communist countries, "virtually all chance of further development has been cut off."

On the other hand, my conversations in places like Macao and Hong Kong, with believers who had escaped out of China, convinced me that while the blood of the martyrs has been flowing in that land as it has perhaps in no country in history, the Church underground is flourishing. My talks with Christians in Russia convinced me of the same. East Germany is on a new campaign allegedly, militantly to exterminate, or at least curb, Christians. But it won't work. On the average, East German Christians are far more dedicated and dynamic than those of West Germany. An interesting article appears in *Molodoi Kommunist,* the official paper of the Young Communist League in Russia. It laments that 60 percent of the babies born in the large industrial city of Gorki are being baptized. This may say little, or it may say much. The Church under the pressure of persecution has always developed a stronger head of steam.

The provinces of Orissa, Madhya and Pradesh in India have outlawed Christian witness, but from my talks with Christians in India I suspect it will only intensify the effectiveness of Christian testimony. The *Saturday Evening Post* the month before its demise had a feature article on *"The Underground Church."* Whether it is in Cuba, Egypt, Poland, or eventually right here in North America, persecution goads the Church into virility and true prosperity. "Be patient, my brothers, until the Lord comes," St. James entreated, for "The farmer looking for the precious crop his land may yield can only wait in patience, until the winter and spring rains have fallen. You too must be patient and stouthearted, for the coming of the Lord is near" (James 5:7, 8, NEB). Let us all pray for the latter or spring rains to fall.

An irony of our times is that while many Church leaders are more and more agnostic, there has never been a time when such a high percentage of laymen believe that a spiritual revival is the need of our hour. *Fortune* magazine's poll of the American people reveals that 53 percent of U.S. businessmen are convinced that a "spiritual awakening is what their nation most needs."

An illuminating statistic is that whereas in 1956, 57 percent of the foreign missionary force of North American Protestantism was made up of representatives of the evangelical denominations and sects, there are now 70 percent and it is rising steadily. "Evangelicalism is where the action is," says the *New York Times*.

I never watch the huge and sometimes almost unbelievable harvest of inquirers stream down to the front in a Billy Graham Crusade, but what I think of the promise of St. Peter as recorded in Acts 3, "Repent therefore, and turn again, that your sins may be blotted out, that times of refreshing may come from the presence of the Lord, and that he may send the Christ appointed for you, Jesus" (Acts

3:19, 20, RSV). Perhaps an accurate slide rule of the increasing harvest in terms of spiritual response, in the 'seventies over the 'sixties, can be seen in the respective responses to the two Billy Graham Chicago Crusades. In the concluding meeting of the June, 1971, Crusade, Billy Graham publicly praised God that the per capita response in the '71 Crusade had been 25% greater than at the '62 Crusade. In the ensuing Oakland Crusade the response was over 100 percent higher than in the 1958 San Francisco Crusade.

The ancient prophet Joel prophesied that in the last days the Lord promised to "pour out My Spirit upon all flesh; and your sons and your daughters shall prophesy" and "your young men shall see visions." Whoever would have predicted in the 'sixties that in the 'seventies — as the organized church gets weaker, deader, and more apostate — we would see a widespread turning of swinging youth to Jesus? *Variety* and *Billboard* magazines claim that as sex and drugs dominated pop music in the 'sixties, religion will do so in the 'seventies, especially songs about Jesus. Already such songs have topped the charts week after week: "Spirit in the Sky" ("What a Friend We Have in Jesus"); "O Happy Day, When Jesus washed My Sins Away," "Amazing Grace," and "Put your Hand in the Hand of the Man from Galilee."

And as we had just about written the youth off to the Devil, along comes a movement of the Holy Spirit among the young which *Look* referred to in early 1971 as a veritable national phenomenon. According to the *Yale Standard*, this *Look* cover story evoked the largest response among its readers of any article in ten years, and two of the three correspondents who went to the West Coast to write it were themselves converted. *Life, Time,* and *U.S.*

*News and World Report* followed consecutively with feature stories on the Jesus revolution.

In a cover story in *Time* (June 21, 1971) the movement is unequivocally linked with the return of Christ, the twelve page article being entitled: "The New Rebel Cry: Jesus Is Coming!" It estimates that already there are hundreds of thousands of "Jesus People," "Street Christians," or "Jesus freaks" nationally, "conceivably many more but any figure is a guess." *Time* goes on to describe its breadth: "Its appeal is ecumenical, attracting Roman Catholics and Jews, Protestants of every persuasion, and many with no religion at all." A California Catholic, according to *Time* exudes: "We are on the threshold of the greatest spiritual revival the U.S. has ever experienced." The prayer of the late Pope John XXIII was cited: Holy Spirit "renew your wonders in this our day, as by a new Pentecost." In late June some "5,000 Catholic Pentecostals from all over the country . . . gather at Notre Dame for their annual national conference." Sociologist Andrew Greely calls Catholic Pentecostalism the "most vital movement in Catholicism right now."

The "Jesus People" movement, according to *Time*, comes amidst a young "generation that has been constantly accused of tripping out or copping out with sex, drugs and violence. Now embracing the most persistent symbol of purity, selflessness, and brotherly love in the history of modern man, they are afire with a Pentecostal passion for sharing their new vision with others. Fresh-faced, wide-eyed young girls and earnest young men badger businessmen and shoppers on Hollywood Boulevard, near the Lincoln Memorial, in Dallas, in Detroit and in Wichita, 'witnessing for Christ' with breathless exhortations." These "Groovy Christians," as *Life* headlines them in a May, 1971, feature article, are in their purest editions Christocentric, crossbearing, self-denying, bold, simple and increasingly Biblical. They are fearless evangelists, being seen, heard, and read throughout North America and overseas. One of their publications, *The Hollywood Free Press,* has a current circulation of 600,000. On national television, we saw 1,158 baptized in the Pacific, and into the fellowship of one church alone. Pat Boone has turned his swimming pool into a baptistry. In Houston, one congregation saw 4,011 make professions of faith in a revival, which was a record, even for a Southern Baptist Church. This was hardly recorded when another revival eclipsed this record, according to *Time,* with an ingathering of 11,000. Teen-agers, as *Life* pointed out, who two years ago would be at Woodstock, in mid-1971 are testifying that the Jesus Way is "heavy but it's not a big spook trip, or anything, like yoga or third-eye stuff; the Lord is just such a turn-on!"

The *Time* article aligns the "Jesus Is Coming" movement with Campus Crusade for Christ, currently having 3,000 full-time staffers on 450 university and college campuses; with Inter-Varsity Christian Fellowship which assembled, at the University of Illinois in December, 1970, a missionary convention of 12,000 (a record); with Young Life, which has 1300 clubs, U.S. and foreign, working chiefly with high schoolers; and with Youth for Christ, which has evangelism cells in 2,700 high schools throughout the world.

I recently was a guest speaker at Asbury College, a Methodist institution in Kentucky, where a student revival broke out in 1970 and spread to campuses across the nation and to peoples around the world. Many thought these revivals couldn't happen anymore. But they are stirring in the mulberry bushes, a precursor among the young of our Lord's promised return. Many denominations are finding a whole new river of blessing flowing into their ranks.

And to demonstrate that the phenomenon is not confined to North America, let us quote from a recent letter written by Anatoly Levitin, a Russian, to Pope Paul VI. He tells of the innumerable conversions of the young of his country to Jesus Christ in a revival which "in intensity and strength is no less than the feeling of fiery enthusiasm among the earliest Christians." Nor are these just peasants — as supposedly in the past. "More and more frequently there are cases in Moscow where the sons of Communists and even of old Tchekists (security police) are baptized" as an outward demonstration of an inner spiritual revolution. Such baptisms in a Communist country require a great deal of courage on the part of the participants.

So the Holy Spirit is at work throughout the world. In South America, last year, the Church was enlarged by an incredible 15% over the previous year. The Church that turns to God in prayer can experience revival today as always; perhaps in a greater measure than ever before — "and so much the more as ye see the day approaching."

# Chapter Six

# Politics and the Coming Christ

The Biblical prophecies concerning the political entities, posturings, alliances, and wars of certain nations, especially as they affected Israel at "the time of the end," are so many, and explicit, that they simply cannot be ignored. Nor should they, when such phenomena as the regathering of Israel, their achievement of nationhood and their seemingly incredible expansion, despite the fact that they have initiated none of the skirmishes which have resulted in their aggrandizement, have thinking people everywhere wondering. For example Charles Malik, Ph.D. (Harvard), the Lebanese statesman who served as past president of the United Nations General Assembly, says that "To dismiss the present conflict between the children of Isaac and of Ishmael (Israelis and Arabs) as just an ordinary politico-economic struggle is to have no sense whatsoever of the holy and ultimate in history."

Other honest questions are being asked, such as: can a militantly atheistic philosophy such as Communism, now entrenched in Russia and China and in control of one-third of the population of the earth, persistently going as far as it dares to exterminate wittingly the faith of Jesus Christ and His

Church, escape the ultimate judgment of God?
China, like the other Communist countries, has
many of the most dedicated believers in history,
living under a regime that is even more hostile to
Christian belief than was ancient Rome. Thirty
million Red Guards boast that they have now suc-
ceeded in closing every solitary Christian Church.
How long can that regime hope to circumvent the
intervention of the God they deny?

Western Europe and North America, as Victor
Hugo has stressed, as a result of their Christian
character, have produced a varied orchard of the
richest fruit in human history. In the wake of Christianity, civilization, culture, education, wealth and
technological advances have staggered the imagination, but the very Christianity which provided a
base for all this is in eclipse. According to the recent
widely publicized Gallup Poll, for the first time in
centuries, every single country simultaneously reg-
isters a distinct decline in Christian belief. As Britain's Archbishop of Canterbury points out, we are
witnessing the advent of the post-Christian era. Can
such a state of affairs long escape the tyranny of an
antichrist? This, especially when it is considered
that, according to some, the Church will be driven
underground or, as in my view, it will be taken
upward into heaven: withdrawn from the "wrath
to come."

Our Lord forecasted that prior to His coming
again there would be "wars and rumors of wars."
(*Wars and Rumors of War,* incidentally, is a book
title for 1971.) It was not only divinely prophesied,
but such leaders as Douglas MacArthur, Dwight D.
Eisenhower, leading writers and the prestigious
editorials of *The London Times* predict a coming
Armageddon with uniform regularity. According to
a standard dictionary, the meaning of Armageddon

is: "Place of a great and final conflict between the forces of good and evil." Will such indeed occur as World War III, as so many pivotally-placed scientists and statesmen are saying?

Obviously only a sweeping panorama of coming events, as forecast in the Bible, is possible here. The *sine qua non* of Scriptural prophecy is the people of Israel. Increase Mather was President of Harvard from 1685 to 1701. In his *The Mystery of Israel's Salvation Explained,* at a time when Palestine was a desolate wilderness, in the hands of the Turks and virtually completely devoid of Jews, Mather wrote with regard to the regathering of Israel to their ancient homeland that "The Scripture is very clear and full in this, that you see not how it can be justly denied or questioned." Mather was so astonishingly perceptive of Biblical prediction that he foresaw that "The Israelites at their return, shall even fly." Anyone who has recently been to Israel cannot escape seeing this happen on six out of seven days in Tel Aviv airport. John Owen, an Englishman, is thought of by many as the foremost of all Congregational ministers. In 1673, he wrote: "The Jews shall be gathered from all parts of the earth where they now are scattered, and brought home into their homeland." An anthology of such statements during every generation from A.D. 70 to the present could be written.

Why should Israel be the special object of Jehovah's regathering? Because God keeps His Word! It is as simple as that. In Genesis we read that God spoke to His friend Abraham, who put implicit faith in Him, and instructed, "Get thee out of thy country, and from thy kindred, and from thy father's house, unto a land that I will shew thee: and I will make of thee a great nation" (Genesis 12:1, 2). When Abraham had obeyed God and left the feathery nest which was Ur of the Chaldees, and had gone into the land which is modern Israel, God again spoke to him and said, "And I will give unto thee, and to thy seed after thee, the land wherein thou art a stranger, all the land of Canaan, for an everlasting possession; and I will be their God" (Genesis 17:8).

When God says, "everlasting," one who believes the Scriptures has no good reason to state that that is not precisely what He meant. Moreover, He promised that such would be His covenant and fealty to Abraham's seed that "I will bless them that bless thee, and curse him that curseth thee" (Genesis 12:3). That the Jewish people are the recipients of these promises was later indicated by the Lord's reappearance to Abraham to assure him, "In Isaac shall thy seed be called" (Genesis 21:12). For 430 years, Israel sojourned in the land of Egypt, but Moses led them back to the borders of their homeland and Joshua guided them in to possess it. After apostasy, during the times of the kings, Israel went into Babylonian captivity, but Nehemiah and Ezra were in the phalanx to lead them back.

In an Israel which had been occupied by foreign powers, since Nebuchadnezzar's siege in 486 B.C., our Lord was born of a Hebrew virgin. A third of a century later, having come "unto his own, and his own received him not" (John 1:11), He was crucified. During the week of our Lord's crucifixion He predicted that "All these things shall come upon this generation." This was unmistakably the siege and utter destruction of Jerusalem by Titus of Rome, in A.D. 70 in which Jews were massacred and those who escaped fled to the ends of the earth, a scattering from which they have only begun to return during recent years. Jesus made it unmistakably plain: "And they shall fall by the edge of the sword, and shall be led away captive into all nations: and Jerusalem shall be trodden down of the Gentiles, until the times of the Gentiles be fulfilled" (Luke 21:24). When it is realized that Jerusalem has been a city occupied by Gentiles until the Six Day War in June, 1967, it is evident that we are living in very exciting times indeed.

Meanwhile, from the time Peter was commissioned to introduce the Gospel to the Gentiles by going to Cornelius and his household, the Church of Jesus Christ has been constituted chiefly of non-Jewish Christians. St. James argued to the Jerusalem Assembly (Acts 15:14-16, NEB), "God took notice of the Gentiles, to choose from among them a people to bear his name; and this agrees with the words of the prophets, as Scripture has it: 'Thereafter I will return and rebuild the fallen house of David; even from its ruins I will rebuild it, and set it up again.' "

In St. Paul's letter to the Romans, chapters 9 to 11 are strikingly relevant. Keeping in mind that in the Acts of the Apostles it is made quite plain that because the Jews had rejected the Lord of glory and crucified Him, God had turned to the Gentiles to regenerate a body of believers known as the Church, Paul taught, "Through their (Israel's) fall, salvation is come to the Gentiles." But this, he states, is a parenthesis. He cautions Gentile believers that they are wild branches grafted into the true tree of God's chosen, but that as Israel has been set aside, so shall she be taken up again: "You will say, 'Branches were lopped off so that I might be grafted in.' Very well: they were lopped off for lack of faith, and by faith you hold your place. Put away your pride, and be on your guard; for if God did not spare the native branches, no more will he spare you" (Romans 11:19-21, NEB).

Paul goes on to say that "It is in God's power to

graft them in again. For if you were cut from your native wild olive and against all nature grafted into the cultivated olive, how much more readily will they, the natural olive-branches, be grafted into their native stock" (Romans 11:24, NEB). Summing up, Paul clarifies, "There is a deep truth here, my brothers, of which I want you to take account, so that you may not be complacent about your own discernment: this partial blindness has come upon Israel only until the Gentiles have been admitted in full strength; when that has happened, the whole of Israel will be saved." Concluding, Paul declares, "God's choice stands, and they (Israel) are His friends for the sake of the patriarchs" (Abraham, Isaac and Jacob) (Romans 11:25, 26, 28, NEB).

The prediction is clear, and the immense amount of Old Testament prophecy pertaining to the final restoration of Israel to their ancient homeland becomes astonishingly meaningful. For example, Isaiah, who devoted whole chapters to this theme, is the Lord's oracle of prophecy: "And it shall come to pass in that day, *that* the Lord shall set his hand again the second time to recover the remnant of his people" from "the four corners of the earth" and "thy people . . . shall inherit the land for ever" (Isaiah 11:11, 12b; 60:21).

Three points here: "again" can only refer to a regathering of Israel since Scriptural days, because the former from Babylonian captivity was the only other one from Isaiah's time to this. "The four corners of the earth," or as Jeremiah 32:37 puts it, "Behold, I will gather them out of all countries, whither I have driven them in mine anger," can only refer realistically to the current return of Israel, because any previous dispersions were merely to one or a few nations in the Middle East: certainly not to anything like the "all countries" in "the four cor-

ners of the earth." Modern Jews have returned to
Israel from 107 countries, literally from all over the
world. As one observer once said, you can find Jews
and Coca-Cola® nearly anywhere in the world. In
China, the most populous country in history, only
28 Jews remain; half are about to be ejected; the
other half, it is reported, are aged or infirm and will
soon die. The third point is, "Thy people shall inherit the land for ever." "I will bring back the captivity of my people," as Amos put it, "and they shall
no more be plucked up out of their land which I
have given them, saith Jehovah thy God" (Amos
9:14, 15, ASV). This indicates that Israel will not be
"driven into the sea" as Nasser so often said. Nor
will Jerusalem again become a part of a Gentile
empire.

The fact arises, that Israelis are moved by chau-
vinism and ethnic ties as much as by an attachment
to Judaism to return to their land. This is true, and
precisely as the Scriptures predict: "In the latter
days," prophesied Hosea, "shall the children of
Israel return, and seek the Lord their God, and
David their king" (Hosea 3:5). The sequence is that
they would return to their ancient homeland, largely
in unbelief as St. Paul taught, and when settled
would begin to seek their Messiah. At the Revelation of Jesus Christ, a "nation will be born in a
day," and as W. A. Criswell, former President of
the Southern Baptist Convention declared at the
Jerusalem Conference on Bible Prophecy, there
would be realized the "happy prospect" that Israel
will "repent over her rejection of the One she
pierced, the Lord Jesus Christ." When our Lord
was about to be born, His coming was to witness
"the fall and rising again of many in Israel" (Luke
2:34). Note the order. Israel would "fall" and be
scattered but they would "rise" again. Histories of

other nations are entitled, "Rise and Fall. . . ." But for Israel it would be "Fall and Rise."

Turning to a précis of events pertaining to Israel's restoration, such a volume of evidence has accumulated over the last few years, and even now is accumulating at such a pace, that the phenomenon almost staggers an objective observer. I happened to be preaching in The People's Church, Toronto, on the Sunday night in June, 1967, when rumblings of the "Six Day War" indicated that the Middle East was breaking into flames. As Levi Eshkol, the Israeli Prime Minister, pointed out, Israel could only get scattered snatches of arms (their tanks were World War I vintage and apparently obsolete). They were outnumbered forty to one, by Arabs with armies that were outfitted with Russia's best and that repeatedly had resolved to drive them into the Mediterranean. In the teeth of these overwhelming odds, I read on that occasion Luke 21:24 in which Jesus stated that when God's time for the return of Christ was drawing nigh, Jerusalem would no longer be trodden down by non-Jews. On the basis of Jesus' statement, I intimated that it should not surprise any Bible believer, if within hours the Israelis were again in possession of Jerusalem, never again to be expelled. In a matter of six days, this and much more was history. The geographical size of Israel was suddenly quadrupled. *Time* magazine (June 21, 1971) acknowledges that the repossession of Old Jerusalem by Israel was a fulfillment to a Biblical prophecy which had to occur before the second coming of Christ.

It was my honor to appear on a Canadian television network program, "Perry's Probe," with Dr. Case, President of the Association of Orthodox Jewish Scientists in Canada. Asked if, as a scholar, he believed in miracles, Dr. Case went into careful detail to point out that the whole existence and expansion of the modern state of Israel has to be a miracle. There simply is no other explanation for it.

The Bible predicted that Jews would be "hated of all nations." How else could you explain Russia's extermination of some six million Jews, Hitler's heinous annihilation of at least a like number in his gas chambers; their being driven, even at this moment, from nearly every country on earth? One of my Jewish neighbors asked me recently, "Everyone is out to get us; why us?" Look at the vote in the U.N. Only twice in my memory has it been lopsided in the extreme. Back in 1956, when the Israeli-Egyptian crisis arose, 71 countries voted against Israel; one, for. When Arab Commandos slew two Jews at the Athens airport and Israel retaliated by destroying 30 planes in Lebanon, on the basis that a man is worth more than many sparrows (even if they are huge metal ones), the Athens incident never got to the U.N. officially at all, but the Lebanon affair did, even though not a single life was lost. Israel was outvoted 101 to nil. Following that, in the streets of Bagdad, nine Jews were hanged and pictures of the massacre radioed around the world. And keeping the issue before the world was the attempt Jews made to get out of Russia back to Israel in 1970, with their trial early in 1971; denied "simply because they were Jews." *The Miami Herald* points to the fact that there has been a strange and inexplicable "disappearance" of more than 100,000 Jews from the Soviet Union in ten years. Senator Claiborne Pell asks why with a half million Jews in Moscow, they are only permitted one rabbi. Former Prime Minister Diefenbaker of Canada asks why the only reporter who was denied a visa to go to Russia with Pierre Trudeau in May, 1971, was a Jew. Frankly, the reason is obvious to

a Bible believer. Is it any wonder that two-thirds
of the Israeli budget is earmarked for defense? And
despite the ecumenical movement with all of its
ironic overtures, Rabbi Emil Fackenheim reckons
reflectively that Christian denominations are more
antagonistic toward Jews today than they have ever
been in history.

What makes the Israeli state more miraculous is
the fact that never in history has a country gone
out of existence and come back in, after a burial of
even 500 years, let alone 2,500. A hundred and
thirty years ago, Jerusalem had a population of
3,000 Jews; and all Palestine, 8,000. Sixty years
ago, there were still only 41,000 Jews in Palestine,
and even after World War II, only half a million.
Today there are over three million, and with ample
land in their possession, and as one of the six nations on earth which produces more food than their
home market consumes, there is now plenty of room
for a rapid increase in population. One has to see
Israel to believe that this land, until recently a barren wilderness, is such a flourishing garden today. In
the words of the ancient Ezekiel, as he interprets
that valley of dry bones parable (given such worldwide publicity in a pop song sung before Mr. Khrushchev when he was entertained in the United States
by Mr. Eisenhower): "This land that was desolate is
become like the garden of Eden; and the waste and
desolate and ruined cities are become fenced, and
are inhabited" (Ezekiel 36:35). As Jan Smuts, a
giant among twentieth-century statesmen, com-
mented, "The greatest miracle of the mid-twentieth
century is not the invention of thermonuclear devices, but the return to their ancient homeland of
the Jewish people" precisely in fulfillment of
Biblical prediction.

The fact that the Jews would migrate back to

Palestine, with the Scriptural conviction that this was inevitable, came very much to the fore among Protestant theologians in the nineteenth century. This paved the way for the political possibilities. Simultaneously, Jews all over the world were fascinated by Theodor Herzl's Zionist Movement, which sought to stir support for a restoration of Palestine to homing Jews. In 1917, General Allenby of Britain captured Jerusalem from the Turks without firing a shot, and in November of that year, the Balfour declaration made it possible for the Jewish people to settle unharassed (at least in name) in their ancient homeland. In October, 1947, sufficient guilt on the part of the great powers, to try to compensate Israel for what Nazi Germany had done, existed to rally support in the United Nations to give Israel a charter to become a sovereign and independent state. The land allotted was slight, but as the hundred million Arabs ganged up to nip the flower in the bud, by demolishing Israel, the first of three miracle-fraught skirmishes took place in which Israel not only survived, but expanded.

So it has happened since, and so it will surely happen again. I was in Egypt on a day when the late President Nasser exclaimed that another war with Israel was both imperative and "inevitable." The *Chicago Tribune* refers to the Jewish/Arab conflict as "irreconcilable." Former Prime Minister David Ben-Gurion assessed: "I don't see any chance in the next few years for any peace in the Middle East." At a press conference President Nixon referred to the Middle East as a "powder keg" that could well lead to a nuclear war. The Scriptures teach that the Middle East conflict cannot be settled, and will not be settled until Jesus Christ comes again. As *Newsweek* puts it, the Middle East is that "perennial chestnut."

"The Bible," asserts Ben-Gurion, "is our mandate." It is not insignificant that the former Prime Minister of Israel, David Ben-Gurion, gave the opening speech to the Jerusalem Conference on Bible Prophecy in June, 1971. In mid-1971 George Cornell of the A.P. writes, "In Italy, it's the opera. In Switzerland, it's the Alps. In Russia, it's the Party. In America, it's baseball. But in Israel, it's the Bible. It's the people's principal pastime." They search its pages for guidance in every detail for the restoration of "the Land."

Modern Israel has only one three-hundredth the population that modern China has, yet this tiny nation gets three times the headlines around the world. Why? Because it is the hinge country on which the world swings. History began in the Middle East and it will end there. There is no point at which Scriptural prediction and current events so exactly coincide as on this Jewish issue. The newspapers are replete with it. Whether you read the headlines, the editorials, letters to the editor, religion or the financial page, plethoras abound such as in the *Toronto Star:* this little land has "expanded beyond pre-1967 Israel's wildest dreams. . . . The country is enjoying the longest and biggest economic boom it has ever known." This takes some saying when one considers such previous eras as those years under King Solomon. And it proposes against all odds to continue to expand. *Time* in June, 1971, quotes Israel's leadership as wanting a million more workers immediately. And while other nations want to reduce their population growth, Israel is working on doubling hers in the next decade.

I shall never forget arriving in Jerusalem on the eve of the first New Year the Israelis had celebrated in occupation and sovereign control of their capital for two and a half millenniums. I have never felt such electric expectation. The air teemed with it. Crowds rejoicing and weeping for joy were everywhere; such exhilaration on the faces of gathering Jews resembled little children as they tear open their Christmas parcels on the morning of the 25th of December in our country. The Ram's horn was ready to blast out the sound that the Messiah had arrived. The old wailing wall, newly excavated and bared down seventeen stone levels, was the scene of indescribable festivities and anticipation! I felt that until that moment, like most Christians, I was unable to grasp what power there is in revived and expectant Judaism. If it is asked whether or not Israel will relinquish Jerusalem again to any other power, the answer of the Premier, Mrs. Golda Meir is: absolutely, absolutely not.

Even interest in a restoration of the Temple is now quickening. The *Washington Post* on May 21, immediately prior to the Six Day War when Old Jerusalem was taken, ran this astonishing quarter-page advertisement, entitled: TO PERSONS OF THE JEWISH FAITH ALL OVER THE WORLD: "A Project to Rebuild the Temple of God in Israel is now being started. With Divine Guidance and Help, the 'Temple' will be completed. It will signal a new era in Judaism. Jews will be inspired to conduct themselves in such a moral way that our Maker will see fit to pay us a visit here on earth . . . Executive talent, administrators, and workers on all levels are needed . . . God will know those desiring to participate." A box number was given. Eventually, according to Defense Minister Moshe Dayan, there will be an extension of Israel's "frontiers to where they belong" to include all "the land between the Nile and the Euphrates." Did Dayan not demonstrate in 1967 that his predictions are as substantial as Nasser's were empty? There is an inevitability about modern Israel.

The Israelis themselves are more and more coming to believe that they are back in their homeland, to await the coming of the Messiah. Christians rejoice in this, believing that the expected Messiah is indeed Jesus Christ. Ben-Gurion and Levi Eshkol have both affirmed frequently that modern Israelis are returning to await the advent of the Messiah. I was listening to the late Joe Pyne, radio-television probist, interview a Jewish Rabbi. Mr. Pyne asked the Rabbi about Israel's real reason for being back in "the Land." Without hesitation, the Rabbi replied that it was to await "the coming of the Messiah." Some people are not aware that one of two lyricists who wrote the rock opera, "Jesus Christ, Superstar" was a young English Jew. No, he does not get Jesus Christ up from the dead, but he does bring Judas back. And the question asked again and again, is the one which Jews will more and more be asking, "Jesus Christ, Superstar, Are You Really Who You Say You Are?" The question is repeated over and over again: "Who are You? What have You sacrificed?"

In late June, 1971, Dayan states, as reported in the *Tel Aviv Yedioth Aharonoth,* that "an outbreak of a new war with the Arabs is inevitable." His former Air Force Commander, Major General Ezer Weizman, at the same time suggests "that Israel should occupy Cairo if a new war does erupt."

Is Russia in Biblical prophecy? I think it is: most precisely in Ezekiel 31 and 39; also in Daniel 11 and Revelation 20. We know from our Lord's explicit reference that Daniel was prophesying specifically about events which would transpire prior to Christ's return. "At the time of the end," envisaged Daniel, speaking from a Jewish geographical perspective, the ruler of "the uttermost part of the north" would sweep down and wage war "like a whirlwind" with "many ships." Russia and her satellites would be the only logical power to answer this description, Moscow being almost exactly north of Jerusalem, and the Soviet Union stretching out 6,000 miles in breadth and 3,000 in depth. "Like a whirlwind" may or may not refer to air transports but "many ships" is not an analogy. Russia presently has the second largest navy in the world. *Izvestia* now boldly remonstrates that the "U.S. Navy should abandon the Mediterranean," as more and more Russian ships move down through the Dardanelles. It was recently announced that Russia now has more ships in the Mediterranean than the U.S., a very new situation. And with Russia obtaining her first naval and air base in Southeast Asian waters — in Ceylon in 1971 — she is entrenched in the Indian Ocean. A great British Naval Commander remarked a hundred years ago that the power which could ultimately gain control of the waters of the Indian Ocean, would best be situated to conquer the world.

Events move with breath-taking rapidity toward their finality in this arena of activity. During the last few days of June, 1971, Bagdad radio announced that the Soviet Union and Iraq (Syria) signed a new pact "strengthening the Arab hand in the struggle against Israel." During the last week of June, 1971, NATO went into special session to consider what to do in the light of the fact that the newly elected Prime Minister of Malta, a leftist, ejects NATO forces to make room for Soviets. At the same time it is revealed that Russia "is building a naval installation and setting up antiaircraft missiles in the Sudan ... some 400 to 500 Russian technicians and 12 to 24 SAM-2 missile launchers are said to be involved. The report represents the first indication of a major Soviet buildup in the

Sudan, Egypt's southern neighbor. Is it any wonder
that *Newsweek* for June 28, 1971 in an article on
"Prophets in Jerusalem" refers to "the conflict between the Soviet Union and Israel, the emerging
battle of Armageddon between the King of the
North and the King of the South — the apocalyptic
adversaries described in the Book of Daniel"?

In the 38th and 39th chapters of Ezekiel, the
details are amazingly explicit. It should be kept in
mind that these chapters follow directly Ezekiel's
vision of the valley of dry bones, which the prophet
interprets, "Thus saith the Lord God; Behold, O
my people, I will open your graves, and cause you
to come up out of your graves, and bring you into
the land of Israel" and "I will make them one nation in the land upon the mountains of Israel."
Then in chapter 38, we read, "Son of man, set thy
face toward Gog, of the land of Magog, the prince
of Rosh, Meshech, and Tubal, and prophesy against
him, and say, Thus saith the Lord Jehovah: Behold,
I am against thee."

There is a linguistic clue that this refers to Russia.
"Magog" is mentioned in Genesis 10:2, and, according to Josephus, his descendants were the Scythians
who migrated to the north, over the Caucasus between the Caspian and Black Seas into what is now
Russia. In the evolution of ancient proper nouns
into their modern derivatives, it is usual for the
consonant sounds generally to remain, and the
vowels frequently to undergo change. So that Rosh
is commonly reckoned by lexicographers to be
Russia; Tubal, is thought to be the Asiatic province of Russia, Tobolsk; and Meshech, Moscow.
M. C. Wren's *Ancient Russia* makes apposite
reading here.

There is evidence again that these chapters refer
to Russia from the fact that, as with the Daniel

passage, their hordes come from "the uttermost part of the north." The atheistic philosophy which impels them would be another indicator. Ezekiel refers to them as "the heathen." A headline in the editorial section of the *Toronto Star* reads: "Stalin's shadow again darkens the Soviet Union." The article shows that the hard line of militarism and atheism are again being followed. And according to the Melbourne *Age* Stalin executed "at least one in every 20." Will such treatment go unjudged? Khrushchev's revisionism is being replaced with Stalin's doctrinairism. Robert Conquest in his *The Great Terror,* a study of Communism in depth, states, "It is now indisputable that the durability of Soviet totalitarianism is structured on the routinization of terror!" Is it to be wondered that such a country has not published a Bible for public procural since 1957? Is it to be considered out of character that Russia persecutes and humiliates Christians with relentless abuse? As "Fiddler on the Roof" portrays, Russia drives Jews out, just because they are Jews and according to a Toronto rabbi, back from a visit to Moscow, "the noose is tightening" on his people there. Is it possible to say God is just and that He would not bring such a regime to judgment?

The ancient prophet Ezekiel states that this power will resolve, "I will go up to the land of unwalled villages . . . all of them dwelling without walls, and having neither bars nor gates, to take a spoil, and to take a prey . . . [from] the people that are gathered out of the nations" (Ezekiel 38:11, 12). This unmistakably refers to restored Israel. "In that day when my people of Israel dwelleth safely, . . . thou shalt come from thy place out of the north parts, thou, and many people with thee;" (the Soviet Union has, or course, many Communist satellites) a "great company and a mighty army: And thou shalt come up against my people of Israel, as a cloud to cover the land; it shall be in the latter days" (Ezekiel 38:14-16). This is a striking statement, but scarcely more so than the one in the following verse, after the explanation, "that the heathen (what could be more heathen than atheistic Communism?) may know me . . . before their eyes. Thus saith the Lord God; Art thou he of whom I have spoken in old time by my servants the prophets of Israel, which prophesied in those days many years?" (Ezekiel 38:17). In short, fulfilled prophecy is always to vindicate the character and authority of God.

Russian Communism baffles its watchers. Winston Churchill sighed, "I cannot forecast to you the action of Russia. It is a riddle, wrapped in a mystery, inside an enigma." When Russia invaded Czechoslovakia (on the day the nuclear ban treaty was to have been signed) the liberal *Toronto Star,* as Canada's largest newspaper, editorially conceded that for several years it had completely miscalculated the policies of the Russians. Canada's former Prime Minister, Lester Pearson, now says: "In my view, Communist leaders have not abandoned their ideological desire to establish Communism throughout the world." Lenin said, "Treaties are only for getting breath for a new effort. They exist to be broken as soon as expedient. Peace propaganda is to camouflage war preparations."

Former President Eisenhower had no illusions about the Russian intent. It seemed to him "incredible that such poison be swallowed, but people who have seen so much political wickedness, cold blood, betrayal and godless depravity in government find it harder to believe our peaceful intent than the clever lies Communism is spreading every, every day."

*U.S. News and World Report* reveals that the Soviet bloc's military edge over the whole combined forces of the West is 2-1 in military aircraft, 2-1 superiority in armed manpower and a 3-1 edge in armor. In one of its last numbers the *Saturday Evening Post* reckoned that modern Israel has no illusions: "What worries them is: the Russians are coming." Rabbi Buben Slonim in his television interviews has given a penetrating analysis of how the Russians are pouring more money into the Arab world than into all their other foreign schemes combined, in an effort to obtain free movement from the Mediterranean to the Indian Ocean, and to procure the oil and minerals they need. Rabbi Rosenburg, the columnist, states that "the real aggressor in the Middle East is not the Arabs, but the Russians." This has been repeatedly affirmed by Mrs. Golda Meir. The mineral reserves in the Dead Sea area are astronomical: an estimated one trillion, two hundred and seventy billion dollars, which is the G.N.P. of the whole American nation for 15 months. The potash alone would fertilize all agricultural lands of the world for several centuries. The most recent boon in the Dead Sea area is an oil and gas find — possibly a huge one. So Russia is not unmotivated in her designs upon Israel.

It is scarcely to be wondered at that Russia does not intend to let a tiny country like Israel stand in its way. "Israel is the only thing that stands between Russia and a Communist takeover of the Middle East," comments the *Miami Herald* in April, 1971. These chapters in Ezekiel, which any careful historian knows have had no fulfillment in the past, indicate that Israel's intuitive apprehensions are not without justification. Milovan Djilas, Vice-President of Yugoslavia and heir-apparent to Tito, wrote in the *Saturday Evening Post* early in 1969 that the

Russian "Party bureaucracy built under Stalin has
not changed much structurally since his death.
Rather, it has fallen into contradictions and troubles
that the bureaucrats cannot solve except by two
means: one is to stifle democratic trends within the
society; the other is to extend Soviet power outside
Russia's borders." Djilas is sure the latter course will
be pursued. He is right.

What follows does not make pleasant reading.
These invaders from the "uttermost part of the north"
sweep down through what has to be modern Syria
"upon the mountains of Israel," and there God's
intervention takes place, which is clearly stated to
have a vindicating effect on His existence and judgments upon the northern invaders; it has a revolutionizing effect upon Israel to turn them to the God
of their fathers. "I will plead against him with pestilence and with blood; and I will rain upon him,
and upon his bands, and upon the many people that
are with him," says the Lord, "great hailstones, fire
and brimstone" (Ezekiel 38:22). Is this the ancient
expression of bacteriological and thermonuclear
destruction? I do not know. It may be. We read that
"I will turn thee back and leave but the sixth part
of thee . . . and seven months shall the house of
Israel be burying of them, that they may cleanse the
land" (Ezekiel 39:2, 12).

Working in alliance with Russia will be the rulers
of "the south" a bloc of nations, of which Egypt
is repeatedly referred to as the leader. It is no mere
happenstance that Egypt under Nasser, and now
under Sadat, has been in the focus of the news so
incessantly over the past twenty-five years. They
don't seem to know when they are beaten. As of
mid-1971, they are making constantly recurring
statements about the extermination of Israel. And
with Russia's newly signed treaty of political, eco-

nomic and military solidarity with Egypt and their pouring of new armaments into that country, the observation of an analyst in *Time* is, "God knows where they're going to put them all." Moshe Dayan reacts that the latest arms buildup is a perilous "worsening of the situation and a matter of great gravity." As the April, 1971, "Federation of Arab Republics" is formed, with Egypt as its head — committed to "no reconciliation and no negotiations with Israel" — even U Thant gasps that the Middle East may well be facing its last chance for peace "in the foreseeable future."

A fourth bloc of nations are the rulers of "the east." They also are referred to in Daniel 11 as converging in the Middle Eastern conflict, the centripetal nation of which is always Israel. In Revelation 9 and 16 these rulers are described as in command of an army of 200 million, these sweeping westward from beyond the Euphrates, which was the eastern boundary of the ancient Roman Empire. It appeared to be an astronomical figure to St. John, but Mao Tse-tung has widely publicized the fact that China now has a militia of 200 million and they propose to use them to conquer the world. *Life*'s John Saar is quoted in *Time* in April, 1971, as getting the impression in Red China of a whole "population marshaled by a military system." "Let China sleep," Napoleon advocated, "for when China awakes let the nations tremble." Biblical prophecy would seem to indicate that the Eastern bloc drives westward in the hope of conquering all before them as a result of an anticipated mutual extermination on the part of the western nations. In the holocaust "the third part of men" are slain. Horrible as this sounds, it is in no way out of joint with what our scientists are telling us. Scriptural prophecy and scientific predictions are terrifyingly coincidental. Only sentimental dreamers ignore the hard facts. One generation ago much of this would have seemed inconceivable. Today, no one but a human ostrich denies the stark fact of events racing toward the precipice.

The prime mover in all this is the antichrist, to whom so much attention is given in Scripture. St. John, who makes several references to him, in his first mention states that in "the last time . . . antichrist shall come" (1 John 2:18). Jesus clearly told His disciples that previous to His coming to earth to judge the nations, and set up His kingdom, men would see "'the abomination of desolation,' of which the prophet Daniel spoke, standing in the holy place"; "Let the reader understand," interestingly interjects St. Matthew. So we turn back to Daniel. Here we discover a man, who arrogates to himself power — wicked, sinister, wonder-working power — and he does just as Jesus said he would do. Halfway through his reign he enters into the Temple of God (by that time restored) and desecrates the altar, thereby breaking the covenant which he had made with Israel, to maintain their peaceful existence.

Thus begins his diabolical dictatorship; his tyranny of terror. He shows himself to have been the most monstrous wolf in sheep's clothing in history, as he sets out to conquer the world. The last half of his dominance Daniel sets at three and a half years, meaning that in all he will be on the scene for approximately seven years after his revelation. "In the midst" of his reign, we read, "He shall cause the sacrifice and the oblation to cease, and for the overspreading of abominations he shall make it desolate, even unto the consummation" (the return of Jesus Christ to the earth), "and that determined shall be poured upon the desolate" (Daniel 9:27). And "from the time that the daily sacrifice shall be taken away, and the abomination that maketh desolate set up, there shall be a thousand two hundred and ninety days" (Daniel 12:11). (St. John in Revelation times it as 42 months.) The antichrist will not so much deny the existence of God which Communism does, as deny His authority. "Antichrist," wrote St. John, "denieth the Father and the Son" for "whosoever denieth the Son, the same hath not the Father" (1 John 2:22, 23).

He "shall do according to his will; and he shall exalt himself, and magnify himself above every god," foretold Daniel, and "shall speak marvellous things against the God of gods, and shall prosper till the indignation be accomplished: for that that is determined shall be done. Neither shall he regard the God of his fathers, nor the desire of women, nor regard any god: for he shall magnify himself above all. But in his estate shall he honour the God of forces: and a god whom his fathers knew not shall he honour with gold, and silver, and with precious stones, and pleasant things" (Daniel 11:36-38).

We see on our television sets super suds, super boy, super light, super mouse, super man, super stars and a *Time* cover feature on "Stars and Anti-Stars." While there is obviously nothing intrinsically wrong with these usages, they presage a pre-conditioning for the acceptance of the antichrist when he comes. Everywhere there is a craving for authority and order. During the post World War II era, more than half of the world's governments have been overthrown by *coups d'état*. On May 9, 1969, United Nations Secretary-General U Thant declared, "I do not wish to seem overdramatic, but I can only conclude from the information that is available to me as Secretary-General that the members of the United Nations have perhaps 10 years left in which to subordinate their ancient quarrels and launch a global partnership to curb the arms race, to improve the human environment, to defuse the population explosion, and to supply the required momentum to world development efforts." The alternative, U Thant says, is a situation "beyond our capacity to control." In May, 1971, he repeated this statement, reducing the time to eight years and insisting that the situation had seriously deteriorated since 1969.

Bertrand Russell said before his death that we must very soon have world government or universal annihilation. He was right. Dr. Spaak, the world-famous statesman from Belgium, expresses how crucially man needs a super-statesman. "The truth is that the method of international committees has failed," he reasons, and "the highest order of experience" indicates that only a world ruler can control the world. "Let him come, and let him come quickly," and "galvanize all governments" and "let him vanquish" anarchy from the earth. Roy Fuller, Poetry Professor at Oxford, argues eloquently how close Europe and America are to a dictatorship. With Walter Lippmann's comment that the world is apparently ungoverned and ungovernable, it was not surprising to see in a recent editorial a portent that, one day, even the Americans may well have to resort to a military dictatorship. In 1971, Senator Fulbright thinks the U.S. is going in that direction. Canada has reached the most critical moment in a hundred years when she could very quickly disintegrate as a nation if no cohesive force arrives on the horizon soon. Her best-known television commentator, Pierre Berton, laments that all the countries of South America, with the exception of Uruguay (and now Chile, where Marxism has taken over), have resorted to militarists as their heads of government as the only way to get law and order, and the trend is sweeping the world. In the so-called "free world" says Berton, "politics has become a hunt for a messiah," quoting as a case in point Governor Hughes, who says as the spectrum of political candidates was being viewed: "I am looking for a messiah, and no one measures up." The sober-minded Cambridge historian, Arnold Toynbee, reckons that man in his present panic is "ripe for the deifying of any new Caesar who might succeed in giving the world unity and peace."

Jeane Dixon, the world-famous Catholic prognosticator, has with interesting accuracy forecast so many happenings over the last few years, such as the time and place of the assassinations of both of the Kennedys. "Believing in Jeane Dixon," remarks a national weekly in 1971, "has become something of a religion in this country." In her *Gift of Prophecy* she claims that the strongest impression by far which she has ever had was the one on February 4, 1962, on which day she is convinced a coming world ruler was born. The Biblical Christian does not, as a matter of principle, put stock in human predictions, but some are quite interesting.

In four of the five New Testament books St. John wrote, he refers to the coming antichrist. In each of his three epistles he uses the term "antichrist" and in the Revelation, where he traces his rise, reign of terror and demise in considerable detail, he calls him the "Beast." St. Paul describes him as the "Man of Sin." History began with the sin of man and closes with the "Man of Sin." As St. John described how he had taught a good deal about the coming antichrist ("as ye have heard"), so St. Paul parenthesizes his description of this coming vile dictator with the reminder to the Thessalonians that when he was with them he had treated this theme in depth: "You cannot but remember that I told you this while I was still with you" (2 Thessalonians 2:5, NEB). So apparently a great deal was said about the antichrist in apostolic preaching.

Before we mention a restricted number of salient features of the rule of the coming antichrist, let us explore St. Paul's treatment of this "Man of Sin" in 2 Thessalonians 2. He is to "be revealed, the son of perdition." "He is the Enemy. He rises in his pride against every god, so called, every object of men's worship, and even takes his seat in the temple of God claiming to be a god himself." Paul further explains, "You must now be aware of the restraining hand which ensures that he shall be revealed only at the proper time. For already the secret power of wickedness is at work, secret only for the present until the Restrainer disappears from the scene. And then he will be revealed," that "Man of Sin" whom "the Lord Jesus will destroy with the breath of his mouth, and annihilate by the radiance of his coming. But the coming of that wicked man is the work of Satan. It will be attended by all the powerful signs and miracles of the Lie, and all the deception that sinfulness can impose on those doomed to destruction" (2 Thessalonians 2:4, 6-10, NEB). The *New Catholic Encyclopedia* (1966) states, "Catholic theologians have been nearly unanimous in maintaining that the anti-Christ will be an individual person . . . The anti-Christ is preserved, for the 'last times,'" his tyranny to "extend" to the second coming of Jesus Christ, who will vanquish and obliterate him, and set up His kingdom on earth.

Who is the antichrist? As the *New Catholic Encyclopedia* points out, all through church history, zealous prophets have audaciously identified certain characters or movements as "the antichrist," only to fall thereby into theological discredit. The same source further indicates, as St. Paul clearly states, that while precursors of the antichrist may well harbinger his coming (a point St. John made by calling these "many antichrists") the real antichrist would not be known until "someone or something" who (or which) restrains the forces of evil in general and the antichrist in particular, is removed. This is, of course, based on the fact that St. Paul says clearly that the antichrist would not be revealed until "the Restrainer disappears from the scene." Theologians through church history have been divided as to whether the Restrainer is the Church or the Holy Spirit. I would tend toward the latter view but either way, the meaning is not altered. On the Day of Pentecost, the Holy Spirit was given in a special way, as Jesus had repeatedly promised He would be, to call out and control the Church of Jesus Christ, and with the "gathering together unto Him" (Christ), the description of the rapture of the Church with which St. Paul opens this chapter, the special gift of the Holy Spirit will be withdrawn.

Thus with all true Christians in heaven with Christ, whether they be Calvinist or Arminian, Protestant or Catholic; of the Apostolic or atomic age: on earth; there will be no "Restrainer." Then and then only will be "the proper time" for the antichrist to be revealed. It is as wrong from both Scriptural and practical points of view, to try and identify the antichrist, as it is to name a date for the return of Christ. Both errors recurringly have brought the preaching of Biblical prophecy into needless and harmful disrepute, and this not just in the twentieth century, but all through church history.

What will be the empire of the antichrist? Most encyclopedias, whether secular, Protestant, or Catholic, indicate that it generally coincides with the ancient Roman Empire, basing this view on Daniel 2 and 7, and Revelation 13 and 17. This would constitute a bloc of ten western nations. According to St. John, when the antichrist is on the ascendancy he will incorporate the power of ten rulers into his own iron hand "to share with the beast the exercise of royal authority; for they have but a single purpose among them and will confer their power and authority upon the beast" (Revelation 17:13, NEB). In his BBC telecasts, former Canadian Prime Minister Lester Pearson has urged a unifying and solidifying of the states of Western Europe, a move which first found pragmatic expression in General George C. Marshall's now historic address at Harvard on June 5, 1947. A year or two ago, it looked as if Western Europe, as drawn together through NATO, was disintegrating again. Now with De Gaulle gone, the Russian rape of Czechoslovakia, and the recrudescence of Stalinism, there is a new craving for solidarity in Europe and a vacuum for leadership, into which a dictator could well step and usurp command.

One of the big political upsets of the latter twentieth century was the election of Edward Heath in June, 1970, as Prime Minister of Britain. For a decade, he has been a passionate proponent of British entry into the European Common Market. All over the world, students of Bible prophecy were electrified to see the *Time* headline in May, 1971: "The Six May Now Become the Ten." By late June, the European "Six" had accepted Britain's application to enter their ranks and with Norway, Denmark and Ireland expected to follow suit, the number would be ten. As *Time* for June 28, 1971, puts it, these countries' entry would give "Europe its greatest unity since the beginning of the breakup of Charlemagne's Empire in 814."

When the antichrist takes over, he will unify the currency, something which De Gaulle in his closing days of power promoted. The European Common Market with its imposing headquarters in Brussels has already taken strides in this direction. Traditionalist Britain and Ireland both moved in this direction in 1971 by going over to the decimal system. In *Time* (June 21, 1971) we read: "One month after the latest international monetary crisis, Cabinet officers, legislators, and bankers on both sides of the Atlantic are intensely debating a lengthening list of ideas" for developing a "global financial system." For many decades Bible scholars have been predicting this.

"In his estate he shall honour the God of forces." The antichrist will be a militarist. In this, he will be like Mao Tse-tung, one of whose sayings is that nothing is useful which does not come out of the barrel of a cannon. The fact that "he doeth great wonders, so that he maketh fire to come down from heaven on the earth in the sight of men" (Revelation 13:13), may or may not refer to thermonuclear devices. But his social structuring strikingly resembles the projected predictions of moderns. For example, after watching a play like George Orwell's "1984" on television, reading Revelation 13 is ominously parallel: antichrist "caused everyone, great and small, rich and poor, slave and free, to be branded with a mark on his right hand or forehead, and no one was allowed to buy or sell unless he bore this beast's mark, either name or number" (Revelation 13:17, NEB). Social security numbers demonstrate this viability. Every newborn baby in Holland, for example, gets a number. There is now a process whereby a number can be imprinted invisibly and irremovably on your hand or forehead by an electronic device and with an instrument can be read at a glance. Increasingly, numbers are replacing names in our world, and while machines are acting more and more like men, men are acting more and more like machines.

It is argued that highly sophisticated Western Europeans would not accept an antichrist dictator.

Evidence that they would can be seen in the mid-1971 Italian elections. There the most dramatic gains were made by the "neo-Fascist Italian Social movement," which received one-sixth of the total vote.

But would moderns actually "worship the image of the beast"? We would have scorned this possibility until Hitler elicited a semblance of this kind of thing. Or take the Beatles: Derek Taylor, their press agent, observed the reaction they evoked in the 'sixties: "It's absolutely rude, profane, vulgar; taken over the world, they are completely antichrist," noted Taylor. "Sick people rushed up. It was as if some Saviour had arrived. The only thing left for the Beatles to do is to go on a healing tour. I'm antichrist, but these boys even shock me." George Harrison can't even have his tonsils out without the hospital receiving hundreds of letters from all over the world pleading for the chance to buy them — or even plastic copies of them. The antichrist will have an abundance of this messianic-type charisma.

An example of how one-sixth of the population of the earth already goes for this sort of thing is provided by Communist China, which has now replaced "The Internationale" with the Redeemer Cult Anthem to Mao Tse-tung which goes:

> The sky is reddening in the east
> This sun is rising
> Mao Tse-tung has appeared to China
> He cares about the happiness of the people
> He is The Saviour of the people.

In Matthew 24, Jesus intimates that when the antichrist desecrates the Temple of God (as Daniel, the prophet, and St. John both indicate, with 3½ years of his tenure left), he will bring such persecution upon believers that it will be a period which

Jesus called the "great tribulation": a time "such as has not been from the beginning of the world." Forewarned Jesus, "So when you see 'the abomination of desolation,' of which the prophet Daniel spoke, standing in the holy place (let the reader understand), then those who are in Judaea must take to the hills. If a man is on the roof, he must not come down to fetch his goods from the house; if in the field, he must not turn back for his coat. Alas for women with child in those days, and for those who have children at the breast! Pray that it may not be winter when you have to make your escape, or Sabbath. It will be a time of great distress" (Matthew 24:15-21, NEB).

Looking for loopholes for unbelief and prodigal living, as man is always prone to do, many at this point ask: is it not possible for me to reject Jesus Christ as Saviour and Lord here and now, as I have opportunity to repent, and then be saved during that period of "great tribulation" to which Jesus referred, after the rapture of the Church to heaven? I do not believe so. For the Gospel preached during those terrible times will be to those who have never heard. Those who have heard and have rejected Christ as Saviour and Lord will fall into the category of St. Paul's description in 2 Thessalonians 2: "The coming of the lawless one by the activity of Satan will be with all power and with pretended signs and wonders, and with all wicked deception for those who are to perish, because they refused to love the truth and so be saved. Therefore God sends upon them a strong delusion, to make them believe what is false, so that all may be condemned who did not believe the truth but had pleasure in unrighteousness" (verses 9-11, RSV). Since this is the age of the Holy Spirit, the unpardonable sin is being committed by those who ignore the Spirit's call to Christ. When Jesus Christ comes to receive His Church, as we rise "to meet the Lord in the air," the present invitation of the Holy Spirit will be withdrawn.

When and where will the Battle of Armageddon be fought? The actual time is indicated by the Prophet Daniel, by St. John in the Revelation, and by our Lord, as just prior to the second coming of Jesus Christ to this earth. It will be, as I understand it, perhaps seven years after Christ's coming to meet and receive His Church in the air, immediately prior to the revelation of Jesus Christ. It will be fought on the plain of Megiddo (also referred to as Armageddon and the Valley of Jehoshaphat), the 14 by 20 mile tract of land which Napoleon allegedly appraised as the most ideal place on earth for a military battle.

"Armageddon," according to the *New Catholic Encyclopedia*, will be the place where antichrist will summon the kings of the earth for the final battle of mankind. The Southern, Northern and Eastern Blocs will all converge to engage the antichrist and his forces. The Biblical descriptions of the Battle of Armageddon are many, and surely among the most dramatic in all literature. "The spirits of devils, working miracles, which go forth unto the kings of the earth and of the whole world, to gather them to the battle of that great day of God Almighty," writes St. John in the Revelation of Jesus Christ, "and he gathered them together into a place called in the Hebrew tongue Armageddon" (Revelation 16:14, 16).

Joel, the prophet, foresaw all the heathen Gentile nations resolve to "prepare war, stir up the mighty men. Let all the men of war draw near, let them come up. Beat your plowshares into swords, and your pruninghooks into spears ... and come up to the valley of Jehoshaphat" (Joel 3:9, 10, 12, RSV). Here Armageddon will be fought. General Douglas Mac-

Arthur, before he died, reckoned: "We have had our last chance. The Battle of Armageddon comes next!"

I was in London the week after the June, 1967, war between Israel and the Arabs. *The Times* carried a remarkable lead editorial on how close we may be to Armageddon, identifying the place, time and combatants of such a war. Mr. Eisenhower replied to Lord Montgomery, Christmas, 1967, that unless peace can be negotiated, then it is Armageddon. *Armageddon* is the title of a best seller. When *Time* is casting about for a word to describe a bloody university skirmish, it describes it as "the Armageddon of the Computer Age." "Will tonight's contest between Toronto and New York be a Stanley Cup hockey game or a preview of Armageddon?" asks Ward Cornell on CBC television in a metaphor all in 1971 understand well!

The antichrist will gain his mandate, not as a warmonger, but as a promiser of peace. Just how desperate people are for peace today is exemplified by the fact that Daniel Ellsberg, a former Vietnam "hawk," was prepared to go to jail for making public the classified Pentagon documents relating to the origin of American involvement in Indochina.

People, from Franklin D. Roosevelt to Twiggy, have said, "I hate war!" Vehement revulsion for war can currently be seen in the United States which has sent 3 million men off to Vietnam. Yet a final war is what man is blindly drifting toward, led by the antichrist. General Sherman said, "War is hell!" Man will end up at his technocratic best and his moral worst. Jesus said of Armageddon, "Except those days should be shortened, there should no flesh be saved" (Matthew 24:22). Pope Paul reiterated during his visit to the United Nations what President Kennedy had said: "Mankind must put an end to war, or war will put an end to mankind." Great men

·agree that man is drifting toward the edge of the precipice.

Will Armageddon be the end of human life? No. Because just when it appears that it will be, Jesus Christ will come. The oldest statement in literature is that written (according to the Apostle Jude) by Enoch, the seventh from Adam, who foresaw this climax of history: "Behold, the Lord cometh with ten thousands of his saints, To execute judgment upon all, and to convince all that are ungodly among them of all their ungodly deeds which they have ungodly committed, and of all their hard speeches which ungodly sinners have spoken against him" (Jude 14, 15). Jesus foresaw His advent to earth apprising His disciples who had gathered with Him on the Mount of Olives: "Then shall they see the Son of man coming in a cloud with power and great glory" (Luke 21:27). For, as Zechariah predicted, "the day of the Lord cometh," when He shall "gather all nations against Jerusalem . . . on the east, and the mount of Olives shall cleave in the midst thereof toward the east and toward the west, a very great valley; and half of the mountain shall remove toward the north and half of it toward the south" (Zechariah 14:2, 4), something which seismologists have known for years is highly probable. In Revelation 16, it is called "a violent earthquake, like none before it in human history, so violent it was" (Revelation 16:18, NEB).

Both for magnificence and glorious truth, there is no more dramatic description in all literature than the following. It previews the moment when (St. Paul says Jesus will consume antichrist with the brightness of His coming) our Lord returns to earth as foreseen by St. John in the Revelation: "Then I saw heaven wide open, and there before me was a white horse; and its rider's name was Faithful and

True, for he is just in judgment and just in war. His eyes flamed like fire, and on his head were many diadems. Written upon him was a name known to none but himself, and he was robed in a garment drenched in blood. He was called the Word of God, and the armies of heaven followed him . . . From his mouth there went a sharp sword with which to smite the nations; for he it is who shall rule them with an iron rod, and tread the winepress of the wrath and retribution of God the sovereign Lord. And on his robe and on his leg there was written the name; 'King of kings, and Lord of lords'" (Revelation 19:11-16, NEB). In the fourth century, Jerome the church father forecast, "No one shall be able to assist the antichrist as the Lord vents His fury upon him. Antichrist is going to perish in that spot from which our Lord ascended to heaven."

As the *New Catholic Encyclopedia* points out, the result of Christ's triumph over antichrist and the forces of evil will be the advent of the millennium, a thousand-year reign of Jesus Christ and His saints of all the ages over an earth which will know unprecedented prosperity and peace. St. John foresaw in the Revelation, as Armageddon concludes with the glorious triumph of our Lord, how God bound Satan "for a thousand years . . . that he might seduce the nations no more till the thousand years were over." Furthermore, he "saw thrones, and upon them sat those to whom judgment was committed. I could see the souls of those who had been beheaded for the sake of God's word and their testimony to Jesus, those who had not worshipped the beast and its image or received its mark on forehead or hand. These came to life again and reigned with Christ for a thousand years, though the rest of the dead did not come to life until the thousand years were over." "Happy indeed," exults John, are these, for "they

shall be priests of God and of Christ, and shall reign
with him for the thousand years" (Revelation 20:2-6,
NEB). "Everything we know," we are told by Willard
Libby, the Nobel Prize chemist, "implies that the
opportunities for future development are unbounded
for a rational society operating without war." This,
I suggest, will be realized during the earthly reign of
our Lord.

From time immemorial, man has longed for a
combination on this earth of law and order; peace
and prosperity; freedom and fulfillment; health and
happiness; godliness and longevity of life. It will
happen when Christ comes again to this earth to
set up His Kingdom. Pope Paul was right, when in
early 1971 he told the Rock Group delegation that
it was "not in my power to abolish war." Only Jesus
Christ can do that. Two New York lawyers, Gren-
ville Clark and Louis Sohn, wrote their classic,
*World Peace Through World Law*. But peace and
law can only happen when Christ comes again.
President Nixon has repeatedly said that he cannot
bring a millennium. But one of the verses upon which
he rested his left hand during his Inauguration address describes what will be some of the features of
the millennium which will be ushered in by Jesus
Christ. This passage, only one of scores which describe the millennium on this earth, is a glorious
prospect for all hopeful aspirants: "In the last days
it shall come to pass, that the mountain of the house
of the Lord shall be established in the top of the
mountains, and it shall be exalted above the hills;
and people shall flow unto it. And many nations
shall come and say, Come, and let us go up to the
mountain of the Lord, and to the house of the God
of Jacob; and he will teach us of his ways, and we
will walk in his paths: for the law shall go forth of
Zion, and the word of the Lord from Jerusalem. And

he shall judge among many people, and rebuke
[many people] ... and they shall beat their swords
into plowshares, and their spears into pruning hooks:
nation shall not lift up sword against nation, neither
shall they learn war any more" (Micah 4:1-4). *Time*
tells us that while the number of the world's doctors,
teachers and engineers is currently increasing only
slowly, that of army officers is rising sharply. The
return of Christ will immediately reverse this. Indeed, there will be no need of the military at all,
for Christ Himself will reign (the solution to the
draft). Then and then only will be fulfilled that
glorious vision of the ancient Isaiah, which no peace
demonstration or human negotiations can effect: "The
government shall be upon His (Jesus Christ's) shoul-
der: and His Name shall be called Wonderful, Coun-
sellor, the Mighty God, the Everlasting Father, the
Prince of Peace. Of the increase of His government
and peace, there shall be no end." And all the world
will commune in symphony:

Our Father who art in heaven,
    Hallowed be Thy name.
Thy Kingdom come, Thy will be done,
On earth as it is in heaven.
Give us this day our daily bread;
And forgive us our debts, As we also have forgiven
    our debtors;
And lead us not into temptation, But deliver us
    from evil.
For Thine is the kingdom and the power, and the
    glory, for ever, Amen.

# Chapter Seven

# Preparation for His Coming

Every time the coming of the Lord is mentioned in the Scriptures, it is used as a basis for the Creator to say to His created, "Prepare to meet thy God." More and more it appears to me that nearly everyone expects to have a showdown of some kind with God, somewhere, sometime. The most outspoken and nationally-heard agnostic in Canada is probably Gordon Sinclaire. As he expresses his sharp disapproval of the *prima donna* treatment a Toronto Maple Leaf hockey star gets from the press, he exclaims, "You'd think it was the second coming of Christ!" Then he adds that he doesn't know why he referred to the second coming of Christ, because he doesn't believe in it. But many of his listeners were not convinced. Instinctively man has always somehow expected, whether he dreaded or welcomed it, an ultimate confrontation with God.

Two days before Jesus' trial and crucifixion, His disciples asked Him those fateful questions, "When will this happen? What will be the signal for Your coming and the end of this world?" Jesus' answer was a 94 verse résumé of signs which when fulfilled would constitute the signal for His return to this earth to set up His kingdom. The nub of the whole trea-

tise swings on verse 44 of Matthew 24, "Therefore
be ye also ready: for in such an hour as ye think not,
the Son of Man cometh." Readiness: that's the key
word, and it occurs several times in the New Testament with regard to the Lord's coming again.

Christ Himself is ready at any moment to return.
As St. Peter puts it, He "stands ready to pass judge-
ment on the living and the dead" (1 Peter 4:5, NEB),
with His wondrous gift of eternal life, "ready to be
revealed in the last time" (1 Peter 1:5b). "The coming of the Lord is near," James exhorted us to antic-
ipate. Indeed, he exclaims, "There stands the Judge,
at the door!" (James 5:8, 9, NEB). Being the most
festive event in history, the second coming is often
compared in the Scriptures to a marriage, our Lord
having gone to prepare a place for us and assuring
us that "the wedding is ready"; or again, "all things
are now ready."

In that believers are to expect the return of Christ
at any moment, Jesus exhorted, "Your time is always
ready." In short, you are to live in a state of perpetual
readiness for My return. This was His message in the
parable of the ten virgins: "They that were ready
went." St. Paul begins his last chapter to Timothy
with the "charge . . . before God, and the Lord Jesus
Christ, who shall judge the quick and the dead at
his appearing and his kingdom" (2 Timothy 4:1), and
concludes that paragraph with: "Now the prize awaits
me, the garland of righteousness which the Lord, the
all-just Judge, will award me on that great Day; and
it is not for me alone, but for all who have set their
hearts on his coming appearance" (2 Timothy 4:8,
NEB). Sandwiched between is the avowal: "I am
ready." As Shakespeare put it in *Hamlet*: "Not a
whit, we defy augury; there's a special providence in
the fall of a sparrow. If it be now, 'tis not to come;
if it be not to come, it will be now; if it be not now,

yet it will come: the readiness is all." That's it. Be ready.

The coming again of Jesus Christ is *imperative*. Man is so fast degenerating within, and so inevitably being dashed headlong toward destruction from without, that apart from the intervention of God, he simply cannot save himself. H. G. Wells and Albert Einstein have been dead for a number of years now, but their observations are only becoming more relevant and solemn with the years. Despaired the former, "This world is at the end of its rope. The end of everything we call life is close at hand." Commenting on thermonuclear weaponry, Einstein reasoned, "The ghostlike character of this development lies in its apparently compulsory trend. Every step appears as the unavoidable consequence of the preceding one. In the end, there beckons more and more clearly general annihilation."

Certainly nothing has happened in recent years to reverse this pessimism. The Canadian physicist, Dr. Allan Munn, says that the thermonuclear devices now with us, "might cause the world and all in it to disintegrate in less than a minute." When Charles Haddon Spurgeon a century ago portended that the world was more likely to sink into a pandemonium than rise into a millennium, he was expressing himself against the prevailing tide, for his was an optimistic era. It was the kind of statement, however, that scientists, statesmen and secular writers everywhere today are making.

Jesus foresaw this with divine precision, when He replied to His disciples, who had inquired about the signs of His coming: "Then there will be great misery, such as has never happened from the beginning of the world until now, and will never happen again! Yes, if those days" were not "cut short, no human being would survive. But for the sake of God's peo-

ple, those days are to be shortened" (Matthew 24:
21, 22, Phillips). So our Lord promises that when
man is about to destroy himself, Jesus Christ will
come again.

A chancellor of Chicago University, where the
first atomic bomb was developed, said, "I cannot see
any future to our known world," and a president of
Columbia University portended, "The end cannot be
far distant." There appears to secular man no hope
whatsoever. Harry Emerson Fosdick, in his balmy
day as the spokesman of modernism, reckoned that
peace was not something which came down from God,
but something to be worked at among men.

Recently a slightly amusing thing happened out in
front of our church. There was a sheet of ice, and
my lovely wife and I were obliged to cross it to get
to our car. Kathleen, from Ireland, not born with
skates on her feet as Canadians have been thought to
be, was gingerly looking down and cautiously pick-
ing every step. She thought that I was just ahead of
her on her right, but someone had waylaid me, and
I had dropped a few paces behind. Into the place I
should have been had strode a man with a clerical
black coat like mine, also on his way to his car, and
walking charily. Reaching out and seizing his arm,
my wife, without looking up, implored, "Darling, let
me hang on to you or I will fall on this ice!" Over-
hearing her request, I accelerated briskly, calling
from behind, "Kathleen!" She thought at first that it
was stereophonic or something. Listening to our em-
barrassed apologies, the startled gentleman gener-
ously commiserated: "Anyone will latch on to anything on this slippery surface!"

Recuperating from the incident, it struck me:
anyone will latch on to anything to keep from
falling on the sheet of ice which is the world today.
And that is just what people are doing. Those who

do not choose Christ and go to be with Him when
He comes again are going to be reaching out in every
direction as conditions in the world worsen. St. John
in the Revelation of Jesus Christ foresaw: "Then the
kings of the earth, magnates and marshals, the rich
and the powerful, and all men, slave or free, hid
themselves in caves and mountain crags; and they
called out to the mountains and the crags, 'Fall on us
and hide us from the face of the One who sits on the
throne and from the vengeance of the Lamb.' For the
great day of their vengeance has come, and who will
be able to stand?" (Revelation 6:15-17, NEB). Winston Churchill wept in the House of Commons as he
reviewed "the awful unfolding scene of the future."
Only the Christian can stand up and be genuinely
confident for, as St. Paul wrote to the Philippians,
"Of one thing I am certain: the One who started
the good work in you will bring it to completion by
the Day of Christ Jesus" (Philippians 1:6, NEB).

St. Paul was certain of the Day of Christ Jesus,
because the coming again of Jesus Christ is immuta-
ble: it is a changeless fact. Affirmed the writer to the
Hebrews, "God, willing more abundantly to shew
unto the heirs of promise the immutability of his
counsel, confirmed it by an oath: that by two immu-
table things, in which it was impossible for God to
lie, we might have a strong consolation" (Hebrews
6:17, 18), a "powerful encouragement to us, who
have claimed his protection by grasping the hope set
before us. That hope we hold. It is like an anchor
for our lives, an anchor safe and sure" (Hebrews
6:18, 19, NEB). I realize that the facts of Christ's
coming are unbelievable for some. *Newsweek* reports
that a poll was conducted across America on who
believed, and who did not believe that man had
landed on the moon. Pollsters were astounded at the
percentage of people who believed that the whole

thing was a staged hoax. Why? Because the physics
of space travel were beyond them. They were not
prepared to take what they couldn't understand by
faith. The fact that we can't understand the astro-
physics of Christ's coming again does not alter the
fact that He is coming.

My ten-year-old son was pressing me about what
the automobiles of A.D. 2000 would be like, and
I told him, as I have been telling you, that in all
honesty, I neither knew what direction car models
would go in engineering or styling, nor whether we
would be in the world at all in A.D. 2000. I was
somewhat ashamed of my incapacity to project that
far into the future, but that Jesus Christ is coming
again I am sure. St. Paul wrote to the Romans:
"Hope maketh not ashamed" and to Timothy, "I am
not ashamed: for I know whom I have believed, and
am persuaded that he is able to keep that which I
have committed unto him against that day" (2
Timothy 1:12).

St. Paul was certain of one thing: the Day of
Christ. Dean W. R. Matthews of St. Paul's Cathedral in London is right in saying that the world is
living on a volcano, not a rock. But the Christian's
hope rests ultimately, not on military defenses but on
the coming again of Christ. St. Paul wrote in 1
Corinthians 3:11, "Other foundation can no man
lay, than that is laid, which is Jesus Christ." The
superstructure the believer builds on this foundation
will be manifest at the coming of Christ. Earl War-
ren claims he always reads the sports section first in
his newspaper because it at least has some cheerful
news: "The front page has nothing but man's fail-
ures." In a world of gloom, man can turn to the
Bible for the good news of Christ's coming again.

A university student who was a star football player
came forward in a Crusade meeting one night to

commit his life to Christ, explaining, "I got tired of playing the game without being able to see the goal-posts." Without a goal, life has no direction. The coming of Jesus Christ is a sure fact, and gives people a goal in life. One columnist, writing of the uncertainties of our times, remarked satirically that the very best our leaders could do was to sophisticate their actions in such a way as to insure that the way to international hell was paved with good intentions.

A sales clerk holding up a gadget pitches, "Here's an educational toy designed to adjust a child to live in the world today. Anyway he puts it together, it's wrong." *Reader's Digest* tells us that even "if all economists were laid end to end, they'd point in all directions." A compass, wherever it is, always points north. So a believer's life always points in the direction of Christ's coming again. "To me the second coming is the perpetual light on the path which makes the present bearable," reasoned G. Campbell Morgan. "I never lay my head on the pillow without thinking that perhaps before I awake, the final morning may have dawned. I never begin my work without thinking that He may interrupt it and begin His own." "Though He tarry past our time," reasoned Matthew Henry, "He will not tarry past the 'due time.'" There is a time, an exact time, on God's blueprinted schedule of events when Jesus Christ is due to return.

The coming again of Jesus Christ is *Immanuel;* that is, "God with us." Both in rapture and revelation, the return of our Lord will be personal. "If God is so wonderful," mused the little Italian girl, "why doesn't He show His face?" That is precisely what He *did* do in the person of Jesus Christ and will do again at Christ's second coming. "Behold he is coming," exulted John in Revelation 1 and "every eye shall see him, and among them those who pierced him;

and all the peoples of the world shall lament in
remorse. So it shall be. Amen. 'I am the Alpha and
the Omega,' says the Lord God, who is and who was
and who is to come" (Revelation 1:7, 8, NEB).
Perhaps John was thinking of that unforgettable
moment when Jesus stood before the Sanhedrin in
the house of Caiaphas, about to be condemned.
Cross-examined by these green-eyed earthlings, our
wonderful Lord burst forth in solitary assurance: that
one day, they would "see the Son of Man seated
[at] the right hand of God and coming with the
clouds of heaven" (Mark 14:62, NEB).

"The Lord himself shall descend," St. Paul assured
the Thessalonians. On ascension day, on the Mount
of Olives, the two white-draped figures who saluted
the 500 upgazing disciples made the point that
"This Jesus, who has been taken away from you up
to heaven, will come in the same way as you have
seen him go" (Acts 1:11, NEB). Bengel, the Greek
scholar, states that the Greek present participle used
here implies that the second advent, as the first, will
be a bodily return of Jesus Christ.

A little girl from the farm was with her parents
riding an elevator to the top of the Empire State
Building. A Christian, she asked at the 86th floor,
"Mommy, does Jesus know we're coming?" One
thing among others is certain in the Bible, and that
is that Jesus Christ knows we're going up to be with
Him forever, because He personally is coming to
get us. Massilon, the historian, wrote that, "In the
days of primitive Christianity, it would have been
apostasy not to sigh for the return of the Lord."
Every time the true Christian goes to the holy communion table to celebrate the Last Supper, he must
focus on the return of Christ to derive meaning,
"This do in remembrance . . . till he come." Every
time he goes to work, he ideally hears his Lord's

words resound in his ears, "Occupy till I come" (Luke 19:13), for "blessed are those servants, whom the Lord when he cometh shall find watching" (Luke 12:37).

The coming again of Jesus Christ is *immense:* the most glorious "trip" man will ever have taken. St. Paul inspired the young preacher, Titus, with the ecstatic aspiration, "looking for that blessed hope, and the glorious appearing of the great God and our Saviour Jesus Christ" (Titus 2:13). Just when it appears that the world is going up in smoke, Jesus said, and man has reached his perigee, look to the apogee: "See the Son of Man coming on a cloud with great power and glory" (Luke 21:27, NEB). Orson Wells has described the perigee. With thermonuclear bombs "we can make a bonfire of all our works, empty our cities, scrape the living crust off our planet, and blast our habitation into a spinning globe of ash."

Queen Victoria left us a beautiful portrayal of the apogee. She was barely eighteen when she ascended the throne of the British Empire upon which the sun never set. Attending officially Handel's *The Messiah* for the first time, she was instructed, "The point at which the Hallelujah Chorus is sung, the entire audience will rise, as has been the custom since the days of George the First. But you are the Queen. You alone remain seated." When the glorious chorus was reached, all stood with military punctuality. Her Majesty alone remained seated. But when that thrilling, transcendent passage, "King of Kings and Lord of Lords," was reached, the Queen rose and bowed, and not a member of the grand audience missed the significance.

Oh, what a day! "One day, Christ, the secret center of our lives, will show himself openly, and you will all share in that magnificent dénouement"

(Colossians 3:4, Phillips), rejoiced St. Paul. St. Peter exulted, "When the Head Shepherd appears, you will receive for your own the unfading garland of glory" (1 Peter 5:4, NEB). "Eternal Glory to the Heroes" was *Izvestia's* prepared headline for the re-entry of the Soyuz 11 trio. But the glory was turned into gloom when the hatch door was opened and the cosmonauts were found strapped in their seats without any sign of life. This tragedy is in direct contrast to the coming of Christ when death will be turned to life and gloom to glory.

As that greatest preacher of the early, post-Apostolic Church, Chrysostom, was dying he seemed to see the vision, "Glorious events; consummation events!" Called out Phil Jenks to his family, "Easy dying! Blessed dying! Glorious dying! I have experienced more happiness in two hours dying today than in my whole life!" S. B. Bangs put it, "The sun is setting; mine is rising. I go from this bed to a crown. Farewell!" Martha McCrackin rejoiced, "How bright the room, how full of angels!" Margaret Prior exulted, "The chariot has come and I am ready to step in." "Eternity rolls in before me like a sea of glory," exclaimed Jordan Ardie. "The One who can keep you from falling," pronounced St. Jude in his benediction, is the One, who on the day of His coming will "set you in the presence of his glory, jubilant and above reproach" (Jude 24, NEB).

I never cease to be thrilled when hearing a congregation sing with Mrs. F. Breck, who though blind, saw as few do: "Face to face shall I behold Him: Face to face what will it be: Face to face in all His Glory; I shall see Him by and by!" The second coming of Jesus Christ is indeed the perpetual light on the path of the believer which makes the present delightful. If Jesus Christ is not coming again, we should close our Bibles and our churches. If we believe that He is indeed coming, the indictment of our being branded as cruel if we are silent is not strong enough language. We ought to study about His coming, sing about it, preach it, talk about it, write about it and spread the precious word of hope everywhere.

Said our Lord, "If anyone is ashamed of me and mine in this wicked and godless age, the Son of Man will be ashamed of him, when he comes in the glory of his Father and of the holy angels" (Mark 8:38, NEB). Someone told me that Eddie Fisher on a radio program recently said that during the course of the day he had discussed everything from ingrown toenails to the second coming of Jesus Christ. If ingrown toenails might be thought of as the low point of his conversation, certainly the second coming of Jesus Christ was the high point.

The coming again of Jesus Christ is *imminent*. No prophetic event or events await fulfillment prior to His coming for His Church. All of the New Testament writers exhort us to be "watching for," "waiting for," "looking for," "praying for," "hastening unto" and "expecting at any moment" the return of Christ. As Martin Luther said, "Christ deigned that the day of His coming should be hid from us, that being in suspense, we might be, as it were, on the watch." The signs to which reference has been made refer primarily to Christ's coming to this earth to set up His kingdom. But His "appearing" to His own in the air to withdraw His Church is referred to comparably often and always in the sense of its occurring at any moment. So we are to be "looking for that blessed hope"; for to "them that look for him shall he appear": not at this time to all; just to "them that look for him shall he appear" (Hebrews 9:28).

St. Paul wrote to the Thessalonians that "God hath not appointed us to wrath, but to obtain salvation" through His Son (1 Thessalonians 5:9). He defined Christians as those who "turned from idols, to be servants of the living and true God, and to wait expectantly for the appearance from heaven of his Son Jesus, whom he raised from the dead, Jesus our deliverer from the terrors of judgment to come" (1 Thessalonians 1:9, 10, NEB). I feel sure that Paul was here referring to what would happen on earth to those who did not turn to Christ, and so would be left to endure the consequent apocalyptical judgments. This same idea is to be found in the Revelation of Jesus Christ where our Lord assures, "Because you have kept my command and stood fast, I will also keep you from the ordeal that is to fall upon the whole world and test its inhabitants. I am coming soon" (Revelation 3:10, NEB). To the Philippians St. Paul admonished, "Let your magnanimity be manifest to all" for "the Lord is at hand." To the Corinthians, "You are not lacking in any spiritual gift" for the exercise of your testimony to Christ, as you are "waiting for the coming of our Lord Jesus Christ." So "be blameless in the day of our Lord Jesus Christ." To Timothy, Paul admonished, "Keep your commission clean and above reproach" for one day you will confront the "coming of Christ. This will be, in his own time, the final dénouement of God, who is the blessed controller of all things" (1 Timothy 6:13, Phillips).

Professor Duffield has pointed out that there are 22 of these quotations in the epistles alone, calls to purity, patience and service in the light of Christ's return. The Church father, Cyril, wrote 1,620 years ago: "Look thou for the Son of God to judge the quick and dead. Venture not to declare when, nor on the other hand slumber, for He saith 'watch.' We are looking for Christ." Adjudged Gibbon, the historian, "As long as this error [sic] was permitted in the church, it was productive of most salutary effects on the practice of Christians." Dwight L. Moody, like Luther and Wesley, preached constantly that Christ's coming was imminent, declaring, "Nowhere am I told to watch for the millennium but for the coming of the Lord." Observed Howden, "Christ's coming is an event fraught with greater demands" than "were required at His first coming." Since Christ's coming is imminent, each of us must at all times be at our best. Nikita Khrushchev promised that "Communism is the wave of the future." The wave of our coming Lord is the expectation of every watching Christian, the wave of welcome which will greet the faithful with the "Well done, good and faithful servant . . . enter into the joy of your master" (Matthew 25:21, RSV).

The coming again of Jesus Christ is *immediate*. There will be no countdown for the coming down of our Lord to take us home. One Greek scholar calculates that the familiar "in the twinkling of an eye" of 1 Corinthians 15, which is read at nearly every Christian burial service, refers to "one trillionth of a second." That leaves no opportunity for the thief to repent or the prodigal to come home. Jesus did not say that His coming would be as a clap of thunder, but "as the lightning." We can with some accuracy time thunder bursts by the lightning flash, because sound travels slower than a supersonic jet, whereas light travels 186,000 miles per second. But lightning comes without a precursor.

"As a thief," said Jesus, and His apostles John, Peter and Paul all used this metaphor. Declared our Lord in His Revelation to John, "Behold, I come quickly," so "hold fast to what you have — let no one deprive you of your crown. As for the victorious, I will make him a pillar in the Temple of my God." George Washington had a cook who was as prompt as the first United States President was truthful. "Gentlemen," said Washington to his guests, "I have a cook who never asks whether the company has come, but whether the hour has come!" "The hour is coming," said Jesus to His disciples, "when the dead will hear the voice of the Son of God, and those who hear will live." All of His disciples of that time fell into that category. Others, Jesus said later, will "tarry till I come." These could include you.

A United States Senator reasons, "The hands of the clock are moving on toward midnight of the brief day left to us." "The clock of destiny," calculates Judge Wilkins, "tells the fateful hour." *Time* notes that "No one is able to see beyond the end of his nose. Profound bewilderment, foreboding, tragic uneasiness, fatalism," are only a few of the traits of our time. "Whom the gods would destroy," goes an ancient Greek proverb, "they first make mad." "If other planets are inhabited, they must be using this earth as a lunatic asylum," bemused George Bernard Shaw. I do not believe that a compassionate Jesus will permit the pressures of an age for which our minds were not designed, to continue to build up until there is mass insanity.

Is there a solution to this humanly insoluble state of affairs? Yes, for the coming again of Jesus Christ is *immigrational*. When does one become a citizen of the kingdom of heaven? When that person is born again. "You," wrote St. Paul to the Philippians, "are citizens of heaven, and from heaven we expect our deliverer to come, the Lord Jesus Christ. He will transfigure the body belonging to our humble state, and give it a form like that of his own resplendent body, by the very power which enables him to make all things subject to himself" (Philippians 3:20, 21, NEB). For this reason, as the apostle wrote to the Corinthians, "we never cease to be confident. We know that so long as we are at home in the body we are exiles from the Lord"; so "we are confident, I repeat, and would rather leave our home in the body and go to live with the Lord" (2 Corinthians 5:6, 8, NEB). Indeed, "we know that if the earthly frame that houses us today should be demolished, we possess a building which God has provided — a house not made by human hands, eternal, and in heaven. In this present body we do indeed groan; we yearn to have our heavenly habitation put on over this one — in the hope that, being thus clothed, we shall not find ourselves naked. We groan indeed, we who are enclosed within this earthly frame; we are oppressed because we do not want to have the old body stripped off. Rather our desire is to have the new body put on over it, so that our mortal part may be absorbed into life immortal. God himself has shaped us for this very end; and as a pledge of it, he has given us the Spirit" (2 Corinthians 5:1-4, NEB).

Ours is a world that groans, as St. Paul wrote to the Romans, groans for the redemption of the physical order; groans for freedom; groans for wholeness. Nina Simone in what soul singer Ray Charles calls, "Message Things," is an international television sensation with her: "I wish I knew how it would feel to be free; I wish I could break all the chains holding me: I wish I could say all the things that I should say, Say 'em loud, say 'em clear, for the whole round world to hear." God's answer to this human yearning to be free and whole is to send His Son.

David Lawrence expresses through *U.S. News and World Report,* "A climax of some kind seems to be approaching the world over." God's climax is the coming of Jesus Christ. Omar Bradley, the American military general, observes incisively, "We know more about war than about peace, more about killing than about living. This is our twentieth century's claim to

progress. Knowledge of science outstrips capacity for
control. We have too many men of science; too few
men of God. . . . The world has achieved brilliance
without wisdom, power without conscience — a
world of nuclear giants and ethical infants." Will the
world get ethically and spiritually better? Yes, but
not until it gets worse, and Christ comes. "The
facts," says *Intelligence Digest,* "show that the forces
in the world struggle are grouping themselves for
a decisive showdown." Man simply cannot better himself. Remarked that senior statesman, Konrad Ade-
nauer, before his death, "Security and quiet have
disappeared from the lives of men." The only answer
is emigration to be with Christ for those who entrust
themselves to Him. When the tyrannies of the Old
World in Europe grew too great, the freedom lovers
emigrated to a New World of freedom and challenge.
Trapped in a world of escalating pressures, one of
these days Christians are going to be raptured to the
glories of heaven.

What is eternally gratifying is that the coming
again of Jesus Christ is *immortality.* Jesus Christ
came "to bring life and immortality to light through
the gospel." When a person repents of sin and
receives Christ as Savior and Lord, Jesus says, "I
give them [you] eternal life and they [you] shall
never perish" (John 10:28, NEB). Along comes Robert
Ettinger, the father of cryogenics to affirm, "There's
no question that suspended animation will work. It's
just a question of when." And so human beings are
being frozen to await a cure for the disease from
which they died. But even this will leave them mortal, subject again to death. Jesus Christ gives us
"eternal life" with a body of immortality. "Lay hold
on eternal life," exhorted St. Paul. Pop songs reveal
how people yearn for a life and a relationship which
will last. "Love Me a Million Years" sings one; and

another, "Forever and a Day"; another, "My Home in the Sky!"; and another "From Here to Eternity." Arthur Clark, author of *2001:Space Odyssey,* said to Walter Cronkite during the CBS coverage of Apollo XI that he craves to live another twenty years and then he might be able to go on living forever. "The moon walk goal is really a quest to live forever," observed that peer of science-fictionists, Ray Bradbury, on the same CBS program, adding, "This has been the quest of religion, politics, and science — to escape death."

We are living in a sad world. "If I were God," ruminated Goethe the German, "this world of sin and suffering would break my heart!" I met Robert and Ethel Kennedy twelve days before the Senator was assassinated. Think of Ethel Kennedy's bereavements: her husband shot; her mother and father killed in airplane accidents; her sister-in-law choking to death at a dinner table — all within a short span of time. Jesus said to His disciples that previous to His coming, there would be "the beginning of sorrows" which would then sharply increase. I saw the actual headline, "The Beginning of Sorrows," in a paper recently. The World Health Organization says that in our world there are 11 million lepers; 50 million with onchocerciasis; 190 million with filiariasis; and 200 million with schistosomiasis. We have already identified Jesus' forecast of famines as a harbinger of His return to earth. In *Famine Nineteen Seventy-Five,* W. and P. Paddock predict that "By 1975 a disaster of unprecedented magnitude will face the world. Famines, greater than any in history, will ravage the undeveloped nations!" What sorrow!

"If there is a God, why doesn't He show?" snaps the agnostic. He will. Jesus Christ is coming and as His Revelation previews, "Behold, the tabernacle of God is with men, and he will dwell with them, and they shall be his people, and God himself shall be with them, and be their God" (Revelation 21:3). And God shall "wipe every tear from their eyes; there shall be an end to death, and to mourning and crying and pain; for the old order has passed away" (Revelation 21:4, NEB). Only immortality with Christ can provide such a wonderful life. "At the moment, efforts to lengthen the life span seem to have broken down," states the *New York Times,* going on to indicate, "The conquest of cancer, heart disease and the like will not lead to a dramatic increase in the life span. Too many weaknesses are built into the human frame to be overcome." What is the answer? A new body in which mortality gives way to immortality. The man was right who said, "Those who take no care for the future, soon sorrow for the present."

The coming again of Jesus Christ is *implicational.* "Yes, I am coming soon," stressed our Lord in the final chapter of the Bible, "and bringing my recompense with me, to requite everyone according to his deeds!" (Revelation 22:12, NEB). Throughout the New Testament, it is clearly taught that when Christ appears for His Church, the first item on the agenda will be the review of believers' works. Thereupon prizes, crowns and rewards will be distributed and status in the life hereafter conferred according to our faithfulness. "For we must all have our lives laid open before the tribunal of Christ," St. Paul exhorted the Corinthians, "where each must receive what is due to him for his conduct in the body, good or bad" (2 Corinthians 5:10, NEB). On this basis, he admonished, "pass no premature judgment; wait until the Lord comes. For he will bring to light what darkness hides, and disclose men's inward motives; then will be the time for each to receive from God such prizes as he deserves" (1 Corinthians 4:5, NEB).

It is understandable then that St. Paul should bring

to a climax that chapter devoted to the coming again
of Christ, 1 Corinthians 15, with "Therefore, my
beloved brothers, stand firm and immovable, and
work for the Lord always, work without limit, since
you know that in the Lord your labour cannot be
lost" (1 Corinthians 15:58, NEB). Similarly, 1 Thessalonians which St. Paul devoted to the dénouement
events, is brought to a climax with the aspiration,
"May the God of peace make you holy through and
through. May you be kept in soul and mind and
body in spotless integrity until the coming of our
Lord Jesus Christ" (1 Thessalonians 5:23, Phillips).
St. Peter shared the same ultimate concern: ". . .
in view of the fact that all of these things are to be
dissolved, what sort of people ought you to be? Surely
men of good and holy character, who live expecting
and earnestly longing for the coming of the day of
God" (2 Peter 3:11, 12, Phillips). Added the aged
St. John, "Yes, now, little children, remember to live
continually in him. So that if he were suddenly to
reveal himself we should still know exactly where we
stand, and should not have to shrink away from his
presence" (1 John 2:28, Phillips). Going on to give
a vivid account of the coming again of Christ, St.
John sums up: "Everyone who has at heart a hope
like that keeps himself pure, for he knows how pure
Christ is" (1 John 3:3, Phillips).

A very vigorous controversy in American government recently has been how much of the G.N.P.
should be spent on exploration of space. Currently
the estimate is 1%. Frank Borman is a potent protagonist of the concept that an escalated emphasis on
space exploration will assist rather than diminish the
solution of the problems of poverty and pollution
here on earth. Jesus taught that an eye to laying up
treasures in heaven would stretch our hand of help
to alleviate human need in this world.

Asked what the greatest thought that ever crossed

his mind was, Daniel Webster replied, "My accountability to Almighty God." "There is no such incentive to evangelism," reckoned D. L. Moody, "as the pre-millennial coming of our Lord. Emphasize what God hath emphasized." In the Presbyterian Confession of 1967, it is pointed out that "The life, death, resurrection and promised coming of Jesus Christ have set the pattern for Church mission." Think of what a congregation like the Peoples Church of Toronto does to evangelize the world. In addition to the hundreds of workers who have gone forth from the congregation through the years, in the present year $430,000 is being given for foreign missions to get the Gospel out to the ends of the earth. What rewards will be forthcoming at Christ's return to those who pray, give, or go forth to evangelize the world!

Christ is coming. What an incentive to evangelize!

Finally the coming again of Jesus Christ is *impending*. Whether the Scriptures are referring to the appearance of Christ for His Church or His coming to earth to set up His kingdom, reference to His return always has attached to it the urgent exhortation to be ready. Oh, the drama and import of Jesus' words! "So shall it be in that day when the Son of Man is revealed." There "shall be two men in one bed; the one shall be taken, and the other shall be left. Two women shall be grinding together; the one shall be taken, and the other left. Two men shall be in the field; the one shall be taken, and the other left" (Luke 17:34-36). "Watch ye therefore," warned our Lord, "for ye know not when the master of the house cometh, at even, or at midnight, or at the cockcrowing, or in the morning: Lest coming suddenly He find you sleeping. And what I say unto you I say unto all, Watch" (Mark 13:35-37). Christian, never let the realization fully escape your consciousness that at any moment Christ may come again. Be always, and do always, those things which would please your Lord were He to come this minute.

In Joel's ancient prophecy we read, "Multitudes, multitudes in the valley of decision. The day of the Lord is near in the valley of decision." In the light of the Lord's coming Joel gave us that Gospel promise which has been quoted wherever heralds of salvation have gone. "And it shall come to pass, that whosoever shall call upon the name of the Lord shall be delivered" (Joel 2:32). To be rightly related to Jesus Christ is to be ready for His coming again.

As Neil Armstrong stepped on to the moon, he declared: "One small step for man; one giant leap for mankind!" The Chinese have an old proverb: the journey of a thousand miles begins with the first step. Certainly the journey to heaven begins with one step: the step of faith which puts our foot down on the promise of the Word of Christ, that He will take to His celestial and eternal home all who on this earth place their firm belief in Him as Savior and Lord. Only that person can join in the final aspiration of Scripture: "Even so, come, Lord Jesus!"

# SCRIPTURE INDEX

# SCRIPTURE INDEX

## INDEX OF PERSONS, ETC.

# INDEX OF PERSONS, ETC.